a,
when
house   1
   to agnes.
   No better woman.

   pages 71 -
      sausage toast (?)
   85 (for my next
         visit)

   and finally, or not -
      page 63
         (bottom)
         t   xxxx

THE BACHELOR GIRL'S
GUIDE TO EVERYTHING

The Bachelor Girl's Guide to Everything

OR

THE GIRL ON HER OWN

BY

AGNES M. MIALL

ONEWORLD

OXFORD

A Oneworld Book

First published in 1916
First published by Oneworld Publications Limited, 2008

ISBN 978-1-85168-583-7

Typeset by Jayvee, Trivandrum, India
Printed and bound in Great Britain by
T.J. International, Padstow, Cornwall

Oneworld Publications Limited
185 Banbury Road
Oxford OX2 7AR
England
www.oneworld-publications.com

CONTENTS

The Bachelor Girl's Guide to Everything

THE INCOME

How to Apportion it.

AT all times, but more especially during the present time, it is a daily matter for girls who have been sheltered and planned for all their lives to turn out more or less suddenly into the world, and be forced to re-arrange their lives at a distance from home and friends. Without any practical knowledge to go upon, they must make the choice between a boarding-house and rooms, learn the intricacies of cooking, catering, hostel life, office etiquette or what not, and find out, usually by painful experience, with what rapidity small salaries melt away. This book is intended as a general guide to do away with the necessity for the afore-mentioned painful experience!

The first point for the bachelor girl to consider is her income and how to apportion it. According to its size and her unavoidable expenses she must make the choice between different modes of living, fix the amount of her dress allowance, and so forth.

By unavoidable expenses I mean disbursements involved by the work taken up, and which, therefore, there is no possibility of avoiding. They vary with the occupation. The office worker has usually her lunches and travelling expenses, the student her tuition and book fees, the shop girl her business frocks, the dressmaker the cost of her various tools and accessories. Such inevitable expenses must be allowed for and deducted before the remainder of the income is apportioned.

Another item which should be decided and subtracted beforehand is:

SAVINGS.

Say that you earn £2 a week, and that your working expenses total 3/- of this sum. Then suppose you put aside another 2/- for savings, and plan your life on the basis of a spending power of 35/- per week. You will then live within that 35/-, and your florin will be regularly laid by.

If, on the contrary, you reckon your weekly income as 37/-, and mentally decide to save whatever you have over on Saturday, the chances are that your purse will then be empty. The only safe plan with regard to savings is to look upon them as a fixed weekly or monthly liability, and to secure them before the rest of the money is spent.

In these uncertain days, the importance of thrift needs no urging. Regular saving, besides sparing the bachelor girl much worry, means the power to hold on in bad times, the possibility of training for a new profession if war removes the present means of livelihood, comfort in illness, and, what many girls will appreciate even more, the ability to be generous to others if need arises. In addition, since all women workers cannot marry, saving also means in many cases the laying by of something for use in old age. Small sums regularly set aside, and allowed to accumulate at compound interest, from the time a girl is twenty or under, mount into a surprisingly large total after thirty or forty years. Until savings amount to at least fifty pounds, the best place for them is the Post Office Savings Bank, where they are absolutely safe and earn $2\frac{1}{2}$ per cent interest each year.

The Choice of a Home.

Having deducted working and saving expenses, board and lodging will claim the greater part of the available income. The smaller the salary, the larger the proportion that must be spent on food and shelter. A girl earning 30/- a week will probably pay quite two-thirds for these two items, while her sister whose salary reaches £3 will not need to expend more than half.

According to the sum available, the choice must be made between the different kinds of "homes from home." Speaking broadly, unfurnished rooms without attendance cost the least; then come, in the order named, unfurnished rooms with attendance (not easy to get), furnished rooms, third-rate boarding houses, a flat or cottage shared by two, hostels for women workers and paying guests in private families. Fuller particulars of each kind of abode are given on subsequent pages.

The choice of a home is greatly linked with the cost of daily travelling, where such is necessary, and therefore the two cannot be considered separately. The individual worker in a big town must make her own choice between paying highly for a dwelling close to her work and thus saving on fares, or adding to a much lower sum for living the cost of a season ticket.

The Dress Allowance.

This item, of course, varies greatly according to whether the post is a town or country one, indoor or outdoor and so forth. Where working clothes or uniform are provided by the employer, less will be set aside for general clothing. On the other hand, girls occupying responsible positions and interviewing many visitors, will be wise to dress rather handsomely in working hours.

Taking the case of a girl who does not wear uniform, and has therefore to provide all her own clothes and who works, say, as shorthand-typist in an office in town, the following figures will serve as a guide. Earning 25/- weekly or under, about £12 a year for dress; earning from 27/- to £3, from £15 to £20. The dress allowance in detail is dealt with on page 96.

Extras of various kinds absorb far more money than an inexperienced girl can credit and the allowance for them must be liberal. Laundry, amusements, odd fares, cleaning, magazines and newspapers, library subscriptions, stamps, national insurance, presents, charity and stray repairs must be constantly met. It is best to allocate fixed sums for laundry, literature, presents, amusements and charity, and not to exceed these limits except in emergency. The other items can be lumped together under a sum set aside for "Extras."

KEEPING ACCOUNTS.

Bachelor girls should always keep accounts. I do not suggest spending weary half-hours to discover the whereabouts of an odd penny; but keep systematic note of all money received and spent. Besides checking waste and extravagance, it is often useful when replacing an article to be able to look up its exact cost.

A SPECIMEN BUDGET

may be useful as a guide before closing this subject. It is the weekly arrangement of a girl office worker who earns 35/- a week and lives in a London hostel, within walking distance of her work.

Salary	...	...	£1	15	0
Partial board and bedroom	...		0	19	0
Working expenses (lunches)	...		0	5	0
Laundry	... ...	...	0	1	0
Dress (£15 yearly)	...	about	0	5	9
Amusements and literature	...		0	1	3
Savings	... ...	...	0	1	0
Presents, charity and "extras"	...		0	2	0
	Total	...	£1	15	0

Unfurnished Rooms.

Many girls prefer to take a couple of unfurnished rooms rather than live in a boarding-house, with its lack of privacy, or be at the mercy of an indifferent landlady in furnished apartments. Unfurnished rooms have also the merit of being cheaper than either of the other alternatives, especially if shared by two friends or sisters, who are willing to wait on themselves. Unfurnished rooms *with* attendance are always difficult, and often impossible, to secure.

It is hard to give anything like an exact estimate of what should be paid for quarters, as their size, locality, convenience, the style of house, and other points, all influence the price. Rents are usually higher in London and its suburbs than in provincial towns or rural districts. The following cases actually known to the author may serve as some guide:

One large front room upstairs in a fairly good road in an outer London suburb, with use of bathroom. Five minutes from station and trams. Sunny aspect, with big bay window. 4/- weekly.

Two small, shabby rooms in poor part of small country town, with good train service to London, sixteen miles away. Gas fitted in one room. No bathroom in house. 5/- weekly.

A very large unfurnished front room upstairs, with small furnished bedroom and use of bathroom. Electric light. Good-class house in superior road in rather an aristocratic London suburb. 10/- weekly.

Two rooms, one fair-sized and sunny, fitted with cupboard, the other small and northerly, with use of bathroom and coal cupboard, in same locality as previous one, but much inferior road, some distance from station. Gas and gas-stove fitted. 8/- weekly.

When viewing or engaging rooms, the following points should be considered:

1. Size and aspect; also outlook, whether to street, over open country, garden, yard or blank wall.

2. Condition of floor, ceiling, wall-paper, window sashes and paint.

3. Lighting and heating arrangements. Size and number of windows, whether gas or electric light are fitted, size and construction of fireplace.

4. If quiet is desired, inquiries should be made as to the number and ages of children in the house (if any), whether other lodgers are taken, if there is a piano or gramophone on the premises.

5. If a daily journey must be made, the distance from the station, buses, trams or tube to be used, their frequency and the fares, should always be ascertained, or the length of the walk to and from work.

6. The presence or absence of a bathroom in the house is an important point. It will rarely be found in country cottages, but town or suburban houses not possessing one should offer lower rent as compensation. If you take rooms in town without a bathroom, you should be conveniently situated for some good public baths.

7. In the country the water supply and the sanitary arrangements should be carefully inquired into. The absence of main drainage is not injurious to health in a properly constructed modern house, but cottages with only outside sanitation should be avoided as far as possible. In country cottages, also, windows are not invariably made to open. Good ventilation must be insured.

8. Most landladies give their lodgers a latch-key. It is always wise to refuse rooms not accompanied by this concession. Insist also upon door-keys to your rooms, so that they can be locked during your absence.

When engaging any rooms, furnished or unfurnished, have a clear understanding with your landlady regarding the length of notice required on leaving. In the absence of any agreement, should the rent be paid weekly, a week's notice is required on either side. When you furnish yourself, however, and moving is rather a big business, it is preferable to arrange for a month's notice to terminate the tenancy.

In rooms of any sort, pay your rent regularly and get a written receipt for the money, which you must keep carefully.

Moving In

may be dealt with here, though it applies as much to flats as to unfurnished rooms. Advice as to the actual selection and purchase of furniture will be found on page 22.

Engage your quarters a week or more before

the date you intend to move in. If the windows need cleaning or the floor washing, your landlady will probably do this for you, or you must arrange with a woman to go in at least two days before you move to do the necessary cleaning. Should papering, painting or whitewashing be needful, or gas have to be installed, ample time must be allowed, as labour may be scarce. Do not insist upon decorating at the present time unless it is absolutely needful, and only attempt to do the papering yourself if you have previous experience of this tiresome job.

If you have not far to move and can run over to the new abode two or three times before you go in, try to get carpets laid and curtains hung beforehand. If new hangings are to be made, it is a good plan to move in a table and one or two chairs in advance, and to measure the windows and make and hang the draperies on the spot.

The actual moving may be entrusted either to a regular removal firm, or to a local man with a horse and cart. Greengrocers often undertake small removals. If, however, the distance is more than a mile or two, or the furniture requires careful packing and handling, it is far better to employ experts. Charges are based on the time occupied; firms will always send a representative to view the goods and make an estimate of the cost. They undertake the proper packing of books and china, and are responsible for their safety. If the move is well managed, it is usual to tip the men before they go away, having put the furniture into the places indicated, unpacked books and china and set up beds.

FURNISHED ROOMS.

This form of accommodation has the privacy which is lacking in a boarding-house or hostel, and the freedom from household cares which one does not find in unfurnished apartments. Furnished rooms may be very comfortable, very much the reverse, or any grade in between, according to the character and abilities of the landlady, and therefore she should be the first consideration when a choice is made. The cost of furnished rooms is more than that of unfurnished, but less than hostel rates, as a rule. Their price includes attendance, and may or may not cover the cost of food. Some girls leave the catering entirely to their landladies, others prefer to market for themselves. An average suburban price for a single bedroom, a sitting-room and full board is (in wartime) 28/- to 30/-. When only breakfast and the evening meal are required, the cost is somewhat lower. Gas or other lighting is included in the price, but coal is usually charged for separately at 6d. a scuttle.

Girls who cannot afford two rooms may take a bed-sitting-room—a cheaper, though less healthy arrangement.

If the house has a bathroom, it is usual to allow each lodger one hot bath a week. This should be stipulated for if the landlady does not offer it of her own accord.

Life in a Hostel or Boarding House.

Here the advantages are that one has no responsibility and that there is plenty of companionship, a fact that appeals to many girls. The drawbacks are that one has (except in the case of the more expensive hostels) no sitting-room other than the public ones used by the whole establishment, that the company is often uncongenial, especially in cheap boarding-houses, and that there are frequently many irksome rules to be observed. For the girl who can afford to pay the terms of a really good hostel intended for educated women workers, however, the life offers many attractions.

The charges made by one hostel in a central London district may serve as a guide for others. For breakfast and dinner, with full board on Sunday, the inmates pay 11/- a week (before the war it was only 9/-). Rooms vary in rent, according to size and convenience, from 7/6 (very tiny) to as much as a guinea. Some are fitted with shilling-in-the-slot gas fires, which enable them to be used as sitting-rooms if desired. All dwellers have the use of the drawing and reading-rooms, library, laundry (where odd things may be washed and ironed), and excellent bathrooms. Hostels in which rooms are shared, or each girl has only a cubicle, naturally charge a good deal less.

The charges at boarding-houses vary enormously. As a rule comfortable board and lodging (partial board only) are not obtainable for less than a guinea a week, and one may easily pay a great deal more. Dwellers in boarding-houses have no household duties, but hostels usually require their inmates to make their own beds and dust personal property. They also have regulations regarding the hours of baths and coming in at night.

Paying Guest in a Private Family.

To become a paying guest is usually the nearest approach, both in comfort and refinement of surroundings and companionship, to the home a girl has quitted. Much, of course, depends upon the family, and it is wise both to ask and to give references before coming to an agreement. The guest has her own bedroom (or bed-sitting-room), and shares the meals, living-rooms, garden and piano with the family. She is generally also included in the social life of the household, and becomes acquainted with other residents in a way impossible to a worker in apartments.

On the other hand, the paying guest has less personal freedom than the lodger or hostel girl. She is thrown closely into contact with the family, and must conform to their hours for meals and other arrangements.

It is not cheap to be a paying guest, though here, again, the cost varies according to the attractions the house and neighbourhood can offer, whether a maid is kept, whether the guest helps with the household work, and so on. The weekly charge, covering bedroom, use of sitting-rooms, full or partial board, lights, &c., may be anything from one to three guineas weekly. Thirty shillings is a frequent sum. There are generally no extras, except fires in the bedroom, nursing during illness, or something else of an exceptional nature.

Sharing a Flat.

The girl worker who can afford an entire flat of her own is so rare that she need not be considered in this volume. It is not at all uncommon, however, for two or three sisters or friends to share a flat, especially if they have furniture of their own. To do so is to establish a home of one's own, and to be entirely independent.

At the same time, a flat or country cottage (the two have many similarities) is rather a heavy responsibility, and should not be undertaken by newly-fledged bachelor girls. Many points have to be considered for which experience is needed.

Flat-dwelling is always expensive, sharing a country cottage rather less so. An unfurnished flat big enough for two or three, and containing a bathroom, costs, in a provincial town or London suburb, from £30 to £60 a year, including rates and taxes, which are paid by the landlord, not the tenant. It is naturally more trouble and expense to run than a couple of rooms, and the wages of a charwoman for two or three hours daily must generally be added to the rent. In addition, the whole burden of housekeeping falls upon the shoulders of the occupants. A flat works best when one of the party is the "homebird," who does not go out to work but assumes the management of the domestic wheels.

Many incidental expenses must be allowed for in running a flat. The cost of gas, electric light or lamps, coal, the laundering of bed and table linen, as well as cleaning materials, must be taken into consideration.

Furnished flats are still more expensive, and tiny four-roomed ones, just big enough for two people, fetch £1 or 25/- a week, exclusive of coal, gas, and household washing.

A COUNTRY COTTAGE.

Hostels, boarding-houses and flats are out of the question for farm-workers, dairymaids, teachers in rural schools, and others whose work keeps them in the country. They have the choice only between living in rooms or sharing a cottage between two or three.

The latter plan has some advantages. By cultivating the garden the food bill can be reduced and fresh vegetables are always available. But the girl on her own must not build too much on what she has read or heard of ideal, diamond-paned, ivied cottages for £5 a year or some equally trifling rent. True, I was offered a residence myself on one occasion for which only £3 per annum was demanded. But it was in one of the remotest spots among the Yorkshire moors, twelve miles from a station, where not one girl in a hundred would care to live; and it had no drinking water laid on, and no sanitation of any description!

Unless the village is very out-of-the-way or the

cottage extremely dilapidated, the rent will probably be at least £10 a year; near a station or if
modern enough to possess a bathroom, it is more
likely to range between £15 and £25. Even the
latter sum is not dear when shared among two or
three. But charwomen are usually scarce in the
country, and dwellings not built for easy running,
so girls adopting this plan should be prepared to
work really hard at cooking and housework, and
to tramp good distances for their provisions. It
must not be forgotten that rates are payable, and
these must be reckoned when calculating the total
cost.

FURNISHING

This is a subject which interests all bachelor girls, except those who live in furnished apartments. Even in hostels such extras as armchairs, desks and bookcases have to be provided by the occupant of the room, and where unfurnished quarters or a flat or cottage are concerned, the girl tenant has everything to buy.

For the woman with plenty of money to spend, furnishing is a very simple matter; I shall therefore deal with the topic here only on the basis that strict economy has to be exercised. As girls starting out "on their own" have seldom saved any money worth mentioning, their capital available for furnishing is generally very small. Probably only absolute necessaries will be bought to start with, and such additional comforts as armchairs, cushions, ornaments and eiderdowns added gradually out of the salary earned. This is a good plan, apart from the money question, as many small points can be settled more satisfactorily after the rooms have been lived in for a while.

The Deferred Payment System.

It may be well to say here that bachelor girls who have no reserve fund to draw upon for fitting up their homes may decide upon the system of furnishing out of their salary. Several firms offer advantageous terms, by which furniture up to given values may be had by the payment down of only about 10 per cent of the total cost. The rest is paid off monthly in fixed sums which can be easily spared from earnings. Naturally rather more is charged for goods on this deferred payment system than when cash is paid, but it enables people to have the use of the furniture at once, instead of waiting months or years until they have saved enough money for it.

The usual rule is that if the monthly payments are not made regularly and in full, the dealers may take back their goods and the amount already paid is not recoverable. A girl should therefore be careful not to pledge herself to the payment of more than she can easily spare. It is also important to deal only with a thoroughly reliable firm; two which can be recommended are Drage's and the Midland Furnishing Co., both of London.

The Bed Sitting-room.

Least furniture is required where a girl has only one room to serve the double purpose of sitting-room and bedchamber; I will therefore deal with this first. A girl with very little to spend will often do wisely to begin in this way, enlarging her domain to two rooms when she has more money for rent and furniture.

One of the first considerations in any kind of furnishing is that of:

Floor Coverings.

The choice lies between

1. Polished boards (if the floor is good enough, which may happen in flats but rarely in rooms).

2. A carpet (either large enough to cover the whole area, or with a surround of stained boards or oilcloth).

3. Cork carpet or matting fitted to the room.

Polished floors are clean, artistic, hygienic, and cool in summer; but they are apt to be chilly during the cold months of the year, and a good deal of work is required to keep them in nice condition. If the floor is not already stained and polished, it may either be done by an expert, who will charge rather heavily, or a girl, with a friend to help her, can do it herself in the following way:

Staining a Floor.

Remove from the boards any nails previously used in fixing a carpet, and scour the surface with a brush dipped in hot soda-water. If the boards have not been stained before, they should first be treated with size. Dissolve two pennyworth in half a pailful of boiling water, and brush it all over the floor. Work as quickly as possible, for the size cools and turns lumpy in a very short time. Let the floor dry thoroughly.

Ready-mixed stains may be bought and applied according to the directions printed on the bottles, but this means an outlay of several shillings. A cheaper plan is to use a home-made solution of permanganate of potash. About sixpennyworth is sufficient to stain the whole of the floor space in a small room, or a broad surround in a large one.

Permanganate stains badly, so mix it in an old pail or washtub, in the proportion of one pint of boiling water to every two ounces of permanganate. Apply this with a flat painter's brush, costing about $4\frac{1}{2}$d. at an oilshop. It is wise to use a second smaller brush when working near the skirting-board, in order not to splash it with accidental dabs. Always brush the way of the boards, never across them, and if the first coat dries too light, apply a second the following day.

When the staining is quite dry, polish the floor well. After rubbing on the polish (see below), a good way of getting the necessary shine is to slide about the floor in old shoes swathed in soft rags. This is less laborious than kneeling to rub up the surface by hand.

Floor polish may be bought in tins (4d.) or made at home as follows: Shred four ounces of beeswax into a jam jar, adding a tablespoonful of cold water. Put in the oven, and when melted add one pint of turpentine, mixing all together to the consistency of thick cream.

Renew the polishing once a fortnight. As permanganate is not a very enduring dye, the floor will need re-staining every six or eight months. A stained floor must be swept over every day, or every other day if the room is only used by one person for an hour or two night and morning.

A stain which lasts longer than permanganate

can be made by dissolving four ounces of shellac in one pint of methylated spirits, and adding brown umber until the colour is as dark as required. This should be applied and polished in the manner already described.

If a carpet is decided upon, it is best to choose what is known as an art square. These woven, seamless, bordered carpets are very cheap, wear well and can be had in many pretty colours. One measuring $8\frac{1}{2}$ feet by 10 feet costs 25/- to 30/-. The colour should be a medium one. Both very light and very dark shades show the dirt extremely quickly. Dark brown, though a convenient tint that tones with many colour schemes, is particularly bad in this respect.

LAYING A CARPET.

Before putting down a carpet, the floor should be well scrubbed and allowed to dry completely. The carpet will wear far better and show the dirt less if a lining of some sort is laid between it and the floor; either an old carpet, carpet paper, or old newspapers six layers thick.

This lining should be spread evenly over the floor, or just that part of it which will be covered by the carpet, for of course none of it must show. If newspapers are used, they should overlap somewhat, or the places where they join may cause depressions in the carpet. Lay the carpet smoothly over the lining. In the case of an art square it is hardly necessary to nail it down; in any case it should not be fixed for a few days after laying. It must have time to stretch first, or it will sag after the nails have been put in.

A stained surround (presuming that the carpet does not cover the entire room) has already been dealt with. The other alternative is to cover the remainder of the floor with oilcloth, which costs from 1/6 per square yard upwards, and needs to be fitted by an expert. It is expensive to lay, but wears a long time, and can easily be kept clean by being wiped over with a damp cloth.

A cork carpet is only worth fixing if the tenancy of the room is likely to be a long one. Its initial cost is high, but against this may be placed the advantages that it wears almost for ever, is warm, and very easy to keep clean. If swept over every day and washed once a fortnight with soap and water, it will always look neat. It is made in plain shades of red-brown and green. Matting is even more expensive, and not so durable.

As little furniture as possible should be placed in a bed-sitting-room or it will be uncomfortably crowded. Generally speaking, it should contain the bed, a chest of drawers with swing glass above, washstand, cupboard or curtained recess for hanging clothes, a fair-sized table for meals, one or two small chairs, a hanging bookcase and one comfortable armchair. If the room is large, other items, such as a writing desk, extra armchair and a wardrobe, may be added. But it is far better to have a room too empty of furniture than too full.

As a bed-sitting-room must be lived in day and night, it is particularly necessary that it should be cheerfully and prettily furnished. The choice of colour will be largely influenced by the wall-paper, but other considerations count. A dark or small room should have light hangings, and the window must not be too much curtained. Small rooms also need small patterns in carpet and draperies, and furniture not too solid or bulky. Remember that striking colours, however pretty they may seem at first, soon weary and afterwards disgust the eye in a small room.

Three-colour schemes are the best, but one of the shades should play only a very minor part, being used, perhaps, as one of the tints in patterned hangings, for an odd cushion or two and for lamp and candle shades. The rest of the room should be fairly evenly divided between the two main colours. For sunny rooms, the cool colours, such as blue, mauve, grey and many greens, are best; cold apartments need brightening with cheery red, rose pink, glowing yellow, and warm brown shades.

The following suggestions may be useful as colour-schemes which experience has proved a success:

1. Dark brown stained floor boards, mahogany furniture, brown bed and table covers, blue wall-paper, carpet, cushions, and eiderdown; hearthrug and mantel-border patterned in blue, brown and pink; pink lamp and candle shades and pottery on the mantelpiece.

2. A girl who took a room papered with violent red toned it down successfully with a light grey

carpet, grey casement curtains, mantel-border and
cushions, black table covers and a red shade to the
light. The furniture already in her possession was
brown of a dark shade, and the pictures very quiet
ones framed in black.

3. Bright blue walls and an orange lamp shade
formed the basis of a daring but successful
scheme, consisting of grey carpet, black stained
boards, black hearthrug, and curtains of chintz
with a black ground, boldly patterned in blue,
orange and mauve. The upholstery and cushions
were partly of the curtain material, and partly of
plain blue that matched the walls.

Soft art green and a dull brown are a good basis
in almost any room. The third minor colour may
be either yellow, pink or pale blue.

In a small bed-sitting-room space (and money)
can be economised by having a combination
washstand and dressing-table, such as is used at
boarding schools.

A girl naturally likes the bedroom part of her
apartment to be as little as possible in evidence
during the day. This is charmingly accomplished
at a certain college for girls.

The rooms have no regular dressing-table, but a
black oak chest of drawers, with a little bookcase above. For toilet purposes a large glass framed
in black is hung over the mantelpiece and serves
by turns as dressing-mirror and overmantel.
Each room has a small shut-up washstand of black
oak, and the beds, which have very low rails, are
spread in the day with dark covers and piled with

gay cushions to give the air of a couch—which they do, very successfully.

A dark bedcover is always preferable to a white one in a bed-sitting-room, and during the day it is easy to slip the pillow into a coloured cushion cover. The washstand can be hidden by a screen, which need be nothing more ambitious than a small clothes-horse covered with fluted casement cloth, and stained black or brown.

THE BEDROOM PROPER.

For an average-sized room you will need:

A bed, with mattress, bolster, pillow, two pairs of sheets, two bolster cases (unless the sheets are long enough to wrap over the bolster), two pillow cases, one under-blanket, two upper blankets (or three if you have neither an eiderdown nor a rug), and either two white bedspreads or one of fairly dark-coloured casement cloth.

N.B. In this and subsequent furnishing lists is given the *minimum* rather than the *ideal* number of items. A girl can hardly set up house with less than is mentioned, but she will do well to collect rather more as time goes on. In this case, for example, it would be more convenient to have three each of bolster and pillow slips, a third pair of sheets and an extra blanket for occasional use. To continue with the list:

A suite of dressing-table (with chest of drawers beneath), washstand, wardrobe, and one or more chairs; or these items separately, in which case perhaps the wardrobe will be omitted.

Washstand set of ewer, basin, soap dish, tooth-brush vase, slop pail and chamber, with water bottle and bedroom tumbler.

Splasher to protect the wall above the washstand.

Carpet, or bare floor with one mat beside the bed and another under the washstand.

Desirable but not essential: fender and fire screen.

A strong iron single bed, with a spring mattress, can be bought for as little as 15/-, but bedding is an expensive item. Cotton sheets are cheaper than linen ones and perfectly satisfactory; they cost from 4/11 per pair upwards. Good woollen blankets are priced from about 12/- the pair up to twice that sum; about 18/- is a reasonable price to pay. Under-blankets are cheaper, or can be made very economically from a couple of yards of wide, coarse flannel, blanket-stitched round the edge with wool. For bolster cases, say from $8\frac{3}{4}$d to $1/0\frac{3}{4}$ each, and pillow cases $6\frac{3}{4}$d. to $10\frac{3}{4}$d.

White bedspreads are expensive and cost a good deal to have laundered, but a hard-wearing coloured cover can be made from seven yards of single-width casement cloth, cut into two equal lengths and seamed together. This can be made for about 4/-, or less if a remnant is secured at some sale.

The suite is the heavy item in furnishing a bedroom and will cost several pounds. Second-hand suites can often be bought advantageously, but there is now a great run on second-hand furniture, and even if considerably knocked about it often fetches very high prices. It is frequently cheaper to pick up the washstand, dressing-table and chairs separately at different shops, and the wardrobe is not a necessity if the room has a cupboard or a recess that can be curtained off and provided with hooks.

Artistic washstand china often tempts girls to spend a good deal of money, but considering its fragility this is hardly worth while. It is better to buy a well-shaped, plain white set; then, if breakages occur, more white pieces can always be got to harmonise with the rest of the set.

Bedrooms are always more comfortable if carpeted, but this is not needful at first. A couple of rush mats costing about a shilling each will wear well beside the bed and front of the washstand. An eiderdown or wadded quilt is a great comfort, and the bachelor girl should buy one as soon as she has an opportunity after getting the essential things. Many girls also like to have a hot-water bottle for use in winter; the stone ones are far cheaper than the indiarubber variety.

Furnishing a Sitting-room.

I shall deal here with the ordinary comfortable room to which a working girl likes to come back in the evening. Of course women who, like those who take in typewriting, journalists, dressmakers, &c., do their work at home, will need to furnish for labour as well as for ease, and with a view to their own particular professions.

The average girl's idea of comfort consists in a pretty colour scheme, one or two thoroughly comfortable low chairs, favourite ornaments and pictures, pet books and plenty of cushions. None of these are difficult of achievement.

Flat-dwellers will probably have their meals in the kitchen, but the first need in most sitting-rooms is a solid, good-sized table to use for meals. Of late there has been a craze for gate-leg tables, and they are certainly picturesque, while in a small or crowded room their folding properties are useful. On the other hand, they are expensive (from 30/- upwards) and uncomfortable to sit at owing to the way the legs are arranged. For real comfort and hard wear, an ordinary deal kitchen table in a small size takes a great deal of beating. It costs about 12/6, or less if bought second-hand.

There is no need for upholstered chairs in a girl's sitting-room. Wooden chairs, cane-seated and stained a dark colour, may be had for 3/- or 4/- each, and are admirable for meals or working; nor need armchairs be a heavy item. A low wooden armchair, with a high back and rush seat, costs only about 12/- or 14/-, and if fitted with a couple of cushions, a square flat one for the seat, and a smaller oblong one to fit into the base of the spine, is most comfortable. So are well-cushioned wicker and willow armchairs, the prices of which range from 8/6 up to £2 2s. 0d.

For the easy chairs get what are known as punt cushions, covered in casement cloth of various colours, piped round the edge with white cord. If bought to harmonise with the room, these simple covers always look well, though the girl who is clever at embroidery or stencilling may like to make more elaborate ones.

With the question of floor covering I have already dealt, but the problem of a fireside rug occurs in most sitting-rooms. Any price may be paid for a rug, according to its kind, size and quality; a guinea is very usual for an Axminster or other pile rug. Skins are not to be recommended, as they are troublesome to keep in good condition. What are known as reversible rugs, made of a strong cotton material and woven in mixed art shades, are most suitable. They usually cost from 7/6 to 10/6 each, according to size.

Most girls have books for which receptacles must be provided. If only twenty-five or thirty volumes are in question, a hanging bookcase with two shelves, costing about 2/- and say, a book-trough at 3/-, will accommodate them all. For the price mentioned the shelf will be of plain white wood, which any girl can stain herself for a few pence.

For a considerable number of books, a tall, standing bookshelf will be needed in addition. I recently bought for 8/- a very narrow bookshelf, only a foot wide, but five shelves high, which just fitted into a recess. It holds about fifty-five books. Or a convenient recess may have shelves fitted by a carpenter, if no ready-made ones will go into it.

Many girls like their sitting-room to contain a little bureau or writing-table. The usual type of bureau, fitted with a let-down desk flap on which to write and three long drawers underneath, is very often to be picked up in good condition at a second-hand shop. Made in mahogany, the price should be from £2 10s. 0d. to £3 3s. 0d.; fumed oak is usually somewhat cheaper.

A girl who cannot afford to buy a bureau may rig herself up a handy writing-table by buying a strong bamboo table (about 10/-) with a shelf underneath to hold books and papers.

It is very easy, when making out a furnishing list, entirely to forget such dull but necessary things as fender, fire-irons and coal-scuttle. As a matter of fact, they are expensive items, and should be bought before funds have begun to run low. The cauldron shape of coal-scuttle usually costs less than the box variety. Best of all, for the lucky girl who has from £3 to £6 to spend on her hearth, is a fender fitted with leather-covered seats. Fire-irons are generally included, and in many cases the seats lift up, revealing underneath convenient receptacles for coal and slippers. If this type of fender is bought, it is usually possible to purchase one armchair the less.

When space is limited, one easy chair may be replaced by a tuffet or pouffe, such as most girls find very comfortable. A large one can be bought for 10/- or less, and has the advantage that it can be tucked away under the bed or table when not in use. It is quite an easy, though rather a tedious business, to make a small tuffet at home, stuffing it with straw or rags.

CURTAINS.

Lace curtains have gone very much out of favour of late years, and casement curtains are now mostly used for sash as well as casement windows. They are usually made of casement cloth (the Sunresista make does not fade), repp or shantung silk.

Casement cloth is cheapest, costing from 6¾d. to 1/0¾ per yard, according to width, the wide makes being most advantageous. Repp, which has a handsomer appearance, usually runs from 10¾d. to 1/11¾ a yard. Shantung silk at 1/- to 2/6 a yard is a luxury, but has the advantage of washing beautifully and being very hard-wearing. Book muslin at 3¾d. a yard makes simple and very cheap curtains when none of the other materials can be afforded.

Curtains for casement windows generally end just above the window-ledges; in the case of sash windows the draperies are nearly always prettiest if reaching to the floor.

Any girl can easily make her own curtains, especially if she has a sewing machine. For each window cut two lengths, the full width of the stuff, and six inches longer than the distance from the curtain-rod to the window-sill. Use the extra inches for equal-sized hems at each end of the curtain. The sides, being selvedges, will not need hemming.

Have metal rods fixed above the windows. The curtains hang from the rods by brass rings, which are sewn to the top hem at two-inch intervals. The rings will have to be removed when the curtains are washed.

If there are no blinds to the windows, and the curtains are intended to be drawn at night, they must be of dark colours, blue, brown or green, should the neighbourhood be one that is under war-time lighting restrictions.

Where there are blinds, and the curtains are not intended to draw, a simpler plan than metal rods and rings may be adopted. For each window buy a wooden rod as long as its width, or cut a longer one to fit. Make the top hems of the curtains deep enough to slip comfortably over the rods, regulate the fulness prettily, and suspend the rods above the windows on brackets or long brass-headed nails. Only single-width material is necessary for curtains which do not draw, and the wooden rods are very cheap (1d. or 2d. each).

Patterned chintz curtains which have a right and wrong side must be lined with a plain material. This goes against the glass, while the right side of the pattern is visible from the interior. Lined curtains are mostly edged with a fancy cord by way of a finish. Looping up curtains is now rather out of fashion, and they are generally allowed to hang quite straight.

Cottage frills at the tops of windows are very popular and pretty. Frills vary in depth from six to eighteen inches, according to the size of the window, and are made of straight strips of material, hemmed at top and bottom like the curtains. The frill should be half as long again as the width of the window.

Pictures.

Pictures add so much to the beauty of a room—if they're properly hung; but ill-framed, badly-arranged art treasures may spoil the look of the nicest house. Framing is as important as hanging, for it may either bring out all the best points in a picture, or, if carelessly chosen, overshadow and ruin it.

It must always be remembered that you frame the picture, not fill the frame. The picture is the main thing, the frame merely its setting, and therefore a frame must never be chosen that distracts the eye from the picture. Everyone knows the kind of thing I mean. Your attention is attracted by a wooden or metal oblong overrun with straggling flowers or a prominent pattern, and it is only after a while that you perceive a print or photograph coyly hidden in that chaos of ornament!

In a well-mounted picture you ought hardly to notice the frame at all, but only to be conscious that the whole effect is just right. If, after seeing a picture which attracted you very much, and at which you looked often, you have no recollection of the frame—then it was chosen with perfect good taste.

It is as well to know what kind of frames are required by different types of pictures.

The heavy and much-ornamented gold frames which our grandparents loved do not go well with many things, but they are the best possible setting for portraits or other paintings in oils. Narrow gilt frames with white mounts inside show up delicate water-colour sketches, and are an effective relief for small, bold, black-and-white drawings. But photographs, coloured prints, sepia engravings and so on, merely look tawdry if framed in gold.

Sepia reproductions should be framed in dark oak, the width varying according to the size of the picture. They look nicest either without mounts or with mounts of the same shade of brown. White affords too glaring a contrast. Coloured prints also look well in very narrow brown or green frames, relieved with a thin thread of gold near the inner edge.

When I say coloured prints, I mean those printed in several different hues. Sometimes you come across very beautiful reproductions, in which shades of soft blue and green are used almost exclusively, giving somewhat of a one-colour effect. Frame these in smooth, narrow black, which throws up the rich, delicate shades.

When hanging pictures, it is far better to err on the side of too few than too many. Arrange the biggest ones first on the large wall spaces, and hang them rather high, with plenty of bare wall all round. As far as possible let those pictures be neighbours which have frames of the same colour.

Medium or small pictures need hanging about the level of the eye—say five and a half feet up. A picture hung over a desk, however, should be on a level with the eye when the spectator is sitting at the desk.

Plain or striped wallpapers are far kinder to pictures than much be-patterned designs. If your paper is quite impossible from a picture point of view, fix a large sheet of new brown paper over the mantelpiece and hang your choicest treasures against this best of all backgrounds.

KITCHEN FURNISHINGS.

Unless she lives in a flat or cottage, the bachelor girl rarely has a whole kitchen of her own. Either she has a little scullery of some sort, or must make shift to do her cooking and washing up in her sitting-room. In either case she has not much room for storing cooking or cleaning utensils. For a girl who lives alone, the following list is sufficient to start with:

Crockery.—Two glasses, one teacup and saucer, one breakfast-cup and saucer, two tea or breakfast plates, two meat plates, two pudding plates, *two small bowls (one for soup, the other as a slop basin), †one or two jugs, †one teapot, *one sugar basin, *one small pie-dish, †one coffee pot (if coffee is drunk for breakfast).

* † See notes on next page.

Cooking Utensils.—One casserole, one frying-pan, one kettle (tin, if for use on a gas-ring or spirit-stove), two saucepans (one, if not both, should be enamel), with lids.

Cleaning Implements.—One carpet broom or brush and one soft broom or brush, or a small carpet sweeper and an O-Cedar Mop, one dustpan, one hearth brush (if there is a coal fire), one mop for washing-up, *three or more dusters, two or more tea-towels, boot-cleaning outfit (see page 92).

Miscellaneous.—One ironing board, two flat irons, one tin opener, one corkscrew, *one grater, enamel washing-up bowl.

THE BATHROOM.

If you live in a flat you will need to spend a few shillings on fitting up the bathroom. It will want curtains, if the window is of clear glass, a cane or wooden-seated chair, a towel-rail or hooks (the former is much better, as it enables the towels to dry more quickly), and a receptacle for sponges, &c. Most baths provide a space for soap, but if not, a soap dish will be needed and should be of enamel. For sponges get one of those light wooden racks which have long handles resting right across the bath, and can be easily shifted to any position. The cost is about 1/3. A small looking-glass will also be useful.

A bathroom floor should be covered with oil-cloth or cork carpet, and provided with a bathmat.

---

* These articles can be bought most economically at a Penny Bazaar; during war the prices of some were raised to 1½d. or 2d.

† Get these items if possible at a 6½d. Bazaar.

This may be of cork, which is expensive but lasts many years, of thick towelling in fancy colourings (costing from 3/11 upwards), or a home-made affair of house-flannel.

To make the last, buy a yard of house-flannel, costing from $6\frac{3}{4}$d. to $8\frac{3}{4}$d., and fold it in half, thus getting a double surface measuring about twenty-five by eighteen inches. With coloured wool buttonhole coarsely all round the double edges, keeping the stitches a short distance apart. If liked, embroider diagonally across the surface the word "Bathmat" in the same wool. In this way you may have a bathmat which answers every requirement for a cost of 9d. or less.

HEATING AND LIGHTING

In towns, the choice is usually between electric light or gas for lighting, and between a coal fire and gas for heating and cooking. In the country electric light is rarely, if ever, available, and gas, though sometimes laid on, is frequently both poor and dear. Recourse must usually be had to a fire for heating and cooking, with lamps and candles for illumination.

A coal fire is always cheerful, and does not dry up the atmosphere as gas and other stoves are apt to do. On the other hand, the heat is difficult to regulate—the fire cannot be let out during a short absence, and will not keep in during a long one; also coal always causes both dirt and labour. If a room requires to be heated for only short periods a day, such as an hour in the morning and two or three hours at night, a gas fire saves an immense amount of trouble. But it is not advisable in cases where heat is needed the whole day. In this case, besides being less healthy than coal, it is an expensive way of heating.

As a possible alternative to coal and gas, there is a varied selection of oil stoves, which serve

very well for occasional short periods; they are
not to be recommended, however, for sustained
daily use.

As regards lighting, most people prefer electric
light when it can be obtained, as it is no trouble,
gives a strong illumination, and does not heat the
room as gas does. It is an expensive matter to have
electricity installed, but if the house is already
fitted it is not a dear form of lighting, as it can be
readily turned out if the room is empty even for a
minute. Electric light should always be carefully
shaded, or it will give more glare than is good for
the eyes.

Incandescent gas is not much trouble, and
generally gives an excellent light, though it has the
disadvantages of heating the room too much in
summer and of blackening the ceilings, unless a
metal disc protector is hung above it. Some people prefer incandescent light to electricity, as it is
yellower and rather more soft. Ordinary flaring gas
jets are very bad for the eyes, and should *never* be
used in a sitting-room in which reading and
needlework are done, though they will serve in
bedroom or bathroom.

In the country nine people out of ten light their
rooms with oil lamps, and there is no more
restful light than that given by a good, well-
tended oil lamp. Girls whose eyes are not strong,
or who use them continually while at work, would
do well to sit by lamplight in the evenings,
even when electricity or gas is obtainable. The
disadvantage of lamps is that they are a trouble to

keep filled and in good working order. (See page 46.)

Candles are mostly used for bedrooms where there is no gas or electricity. Though not to be recommended for regular working use, a pair of candles, properly fitted with shades, which conceal their flickering from the eyes, makes a good desk or piano light, if placed about a foot higher than the work. It is most injurious to the eyes to read or sew for any length of time by the light of a single, unshaded candle.

Candles of the usual size now cost as much as 8d. per pound (usually one dozen), and a pair will burn right through in about two and a half or three hours. Therefore economy in their use is necessary, and the stumps should never be thrown away. It is a good plan, when a candle has burnt right down to the candlestick socket, to cut off the wick and trim it level with a pen-knife. Then the next candle can be fixed to the stump by melting the wax a little, and so will burn right down to the end without going out.

Hints about Gas Burners.

Gas burners will not give a satisfactory light unless they are kept free from dust; it is also very important that the globe should be kept clean. Wipe them over frequently with a slightly damp duster, and every few months remove them and give a thorough washing in hot water. When replacing a globe, be very careful only to screw it just tightly enough to keep it from falling.

If fixed too tightly, it will probably crack soon after the gas is lighted, as the heat causes the glass to expand and take up more space.

When a new mantle needs fitting, be careful not to touch the fragile white part, or you will probably make a hole in it and injure your light. The mantle should be handled by the little metal or porcelain bit at the top.

A strong smell of gas at any time indicates a leakage somewhere. In this case it is risky to take a light to the suspected spot. Instead, open all the doors and windows, turn off the gas at the meter, and then examine all the taps. One may have been left on, thus causing the smell, but if all are properly turned off there must be a leakage in the pipes, and a gasfitter should be sent for to repair the damage. If he delays coming, and it is necessary to use the gas in the meantime, turn it on and run a lighted taper along the pipes. At the spot where the leakage is occurring the gas will light. Turn off the gas, and plug the leak temporarily with soap.

For the management of gas *cookers* see page 54.

The Care of a Lamp.

Some people have an idea that lamps are dangerous, but this is far from being the case if they are properly made, and oil of good quality is used. Accidents with lamps, as with knives or other household implements, are generally the result of carelessness.

A safe lamp which will give a good light ought

not to cost more than 5/- or 6/-, though much higher prices may be paid for design and ornament, as distinct from security. The lamp is perhaps the cheapest of all forms of lighting, and as it is portable it may be used in one room or another, as required.

A lamp should have a broad, heavy base, so that there is no risk of its being overturned, and the wick should fit well. It should also have an extinguisher, as the practice of blowing out a lamp is not to be recommended; a safer alternative if there is no extinguisher is to turn down the wick, at the same time holding a metal tray over the top of the chimney until the light goes out.

If a lamp is in daily use it will require trimming every day—a process which should be done in daylight, right away from a fire.

To trim a lamp stand it on a sheet of newspaper, dust it, and remove and clean the globe and chimney. Fill the reservoir two-thirds full of oil; if entirely filled the oil is apt to drip about. Turn the wick right down, so that only the charred edge of it shows above the holder, and if this is rough rub it down level with a crumpled piece of paper. Never *cut* a wick. Wipe the lamp over with paper to remove any stray drops of oil, and then rub with a soft duster.

Many good lamps have a little handle by which the globe and chimney can be raised out of the way while the wick is lighted, but if this is not the case, they must be removed. Turn the wick low before lighting, then put the match to it and replace the glass parts. Let the wick burn for a few minutes before turning it up, to minimise the risk of cracking the chimney. A chimney is less likely to come to grief in this way if, before being used, it has been wrapped in a soft old rag and boiled for half an hour. It must be left in the water until the latter has entirely cooled. A chimney is also apt to crack unless it is put on perfectly straight.

If a lamp burns badly it may need cleaning. About once a month it is advisable to boil the burner for a few minutes in hot soda water; then rinse in clean water and dry before replacing in the lamp. A special old saucepan or tin must be kept for this job.

Always use the very best paraffin. The lower-priced varieties, being often imperfectly purified, are dangerous to use and may cause an explosion. Saving on the cost of paraffin oil is economy of the falsest description.

If, in spite of all care, a lamp is overturned, and any of the contents of the room set on fire, the flames must be extinguished with earth, sand or flour, or by throwing a rug, woollen curtain or some similar heavy article over the conflagration. In such a case water is worse than useless, as the oil floats on it, and thus spreads the flames.

Hints regarding the management of oil stoves will be found on page 57.

CATERING

It is unfortunate that the bachelor girl, setting up housekeeping in most cases with no experience to guide her, is confronted with the most difficult kind of catering—that for one person only, or perhaps two. Owing to the fact that everything must be bought in small quantities, many foods, especially meat dishes, must be entirely ruled out, and consequently it is difficult to make the menu sufficiently varied.

The following general suggestions will be helpful, and the recipes given on page 68 and the following pages, have all been specially chosen for one or two people.

Tinned foods (dealt with more fully under "The Emergency Cupboard") besides being somewhat expensive, are not satisfactory nourishment for daily use, though often useful on special occasions. Ready-prepared custard and jelly powders, however, soups in cubes and such things as Oxo and Ivelcon, may be used as often as desired without injurious effects, and save a good deal of tiresome cooking.

In nine cases out of ten, bachelor girls do not have to prepare their midday meal; breakfast and supper (or dinner) are the repasts with which they mainly have to deal. Portable lunches, taken to and eaten at work, are dealt with on page 64, and serve as equally good suggestions for the rare girl who comes home at midday and gets her own meal.

In the establishment for one or two, joints are too big to have a place, but the meat course is varied if chops, steak, fish, eggs, sausages, ready-cooked ham, tongue and corned beef, are pressed into service. Small pieces of meat left over from a meal are appetising served the next day in the form of croquettes or rissoles. A young rabbit will provide two tempting suppers for two people.

Eggs boiled, poached or served in one of the ways given among the recipes on page 74 are always a welcome change for breakfast or supper, and suggestions will also be found for delicious fish dishes, while the menu may be varied occasionally (not oftener than once a week) by a "tinned" meal of sardines, salmon or herrings with tomato sauce. It is a good plan to have the weekly "tinned" repast on a specially tiring or busy day, as it saves so much trouble. In cold weather, provide the heat lacking in tinned preparations by taking first a cupful of hot soup, Oxo or Ivelcon, or the two last mixed in equal quantities.

Vegetarian dishes have gained in favour enormously since the war, and have the advantage that they can be prepared in large or small quantities, to suit a party of any size. Recipes will be found on page 75, and any good cookery book, costing only a few pence, will provide suggestions for many more satisfactory dishes.

To save trouble, when boiling potatoes prepare a double quantity. What are left over can be fried the next day or made up with scraps of cold meat into tasty croquettes. Green vegetables are important to health, and it is very unwise to shirk the extra trouble of cooking them. Salads, which do not need any cooking, may often be served; they help to purify the blood.

Fruit is just as valuable to health as green-stuff, and here again, enough may be stewed to last for two or three meals. It is easy to vary the monotony by serving it on one occasion with a little cream, on another with custard, and a third with plain boiled rice or junket (made with warm milk and rennet powder, according to the directions on the bottle).

Cream need not be specially bought to provide the small quantity required for one or two people, when served with fruit or a sweet dish. A pint of milk, set to stand in a bowl in the morning before going to work, will yield a tiny jugful of cream if skimmed at supper-time. The milk remaining may be used for milk puddings and porridge.

It is a dainty idea to make puddings for one or two, when these require to be set in a mould, in small bowls or breakfast cups. It is much more attractive to demolish one small pudding each time than to go on with the remains of a large one.

A girl living alone should always take pains to set her table attractively, in order to stimulate her appetite, which generally suffers when meals are consumed in solitude. Keep your silver and table linen fresh and clean and set a few flowers or a little fern on the board. It is surprising how much difference is made by these apparent trifles.

Shopping Hints.

Girls who are out most of the day cannot give orders at the door and have them delivered an hour or two later. Shopping must be done in person and purchases carried home. Though this is sometimes burdensome, it is really a blessing in disguise when funds are strictly limited, as one is able to see what is cheap (not much nowadays!) and to shop much more advantageously.

It is wiser not to have accounts with tradespeople, but to pay for everything as it is bought. Not only do you get goods cheaper in this way, as the shop folk are saved the bother of booking them, but you avoid the risk of delaying payment until the bills are big enough to be a serious worry. "Cash down" is a good bachelor girl motto.

If you live in the country, with no good shops near, and your work takes you into a town every day, you will be able to get much foodstuff at the big shops, where there is more variety. Local country products, however, such as sausages, greenstuff, eggs, butter and cream, are usually cheaper, and certainly fresher, if purchased near home.

The Emergency Cupboard.

Every bachelor girl who has a little space for storage is well advised to keep a supply of tinned and concentrated foods. Not only are they invaluable if a visitor arrives unexpectedly, but they form a reserve to draw upon if, through bad weather, lack of time or any other cause, a girl cannot do her usual marketing. Emergency foods, being mostly rather expensive, should, however, be reserved strictly for use on exceptional occasions, and not taken out of store at any time to save a little bother.

The store cupboard should always contain a tin of condensed milk, so useful if tea is needed unusually early or late, when fresh milk is not forthcoming; a quarter of a pound of plain biscuits, packets of jelly, blancmange and custard powders, cubes of soup, a pot of jam, a tin of shortbread (in case a friend drops in to tea on Sunday) tinned salmon and sardines and a tin of apricots, peaches or pineapple chunks; also a bottle of rennet.

These are the more everyday requirements, but many other foods may be had in tins or bottles, ready to serve, and some of these may well find a place upon the emergency shelf: spaghetti and tomato with cheese, peas, beans and asparagus in bottles, tongue in glass jars, flaked fish, kippered herrings, boneless mackerel, brawn, devilled ham, spiced beef, minced steak, tomato purée (for making soups and sauces), fish and meat pastes in various flavours, tinned and bottled fruit of every description and so forth.

Directly a tin is opened, the contents must be emptied out on to a dish. If left-over portions remain in the tin until another day, a serious risk is run of their becoming unfit for food and causing grave illness. An unopened tin which *bulges* should never be used, as the bulge indicates that the contents of the tin have deteriorated and become unfit to eat. Goods packed in glass jars or bottles may safely remain in them until entirely consumed.

MANAGING A GAS STOVE.

There is no more convenient kind of cooker for the bachelor girl than the gas stove, which is clean, can be lighted in a moment and has heat much more easily regulated than is the case with a coal range. If the rooms taken have no stove fitted, one may easily be hired from the local gas company. The cost is very slight, usually about 2/6d. per quarter for a medium-sized stove. It can also be got on the hire purchase system, by which the cost of the stove is paid off as rent in quarterly instalments, and ultimately becomes the hirer's property. Hot water geysers can be bought on the same terms, and are very convenient in flats.

If a stove is fitted for heating purposes, not primarily for cooking, one should be chosen that has a ring at the side or on the top, on which a kettle can be boiled. A gas grill, most convenient for quickly cooking chops, bacon, eggs, etc. or making toast, is a very useful adjunct to bachelor girl cookery. The gas must be allowed to heat it thoroughly before the food is put underneath.

If properly managed, a gas stove is quite odourless. The gassy smell which pervades many households is caused by the stove not being kept perfectly clean. Dirt also clogs up the burners and causes waste of heat.

A gas oven is lined with enamel, and if this is wiped over after each use with a damp sponge, it will always be spotlessly white. Once a week the whole stove should be washed with plenty of very hot water containing soda, all the movable parts being removed for the purpose. Then the burners must be cleaned with a small stiff brush, washed, and blackleaded with the other black parts of the stove, the taps polished and all steel portions rubbed up with emery paper.

If a scrupulously clean stove smells, this indicates an escape of gas somewhere, and the gas company should be notified at once.

Should food be spilt or boil over during cooking, it must be wiped off at once with a cloth wrung out of warm water. Dirty tins and pans should never be left standing on the stove after use. Leave the oven door open when baking is over, so that the odour of, say, the meat which has just been cooked, will not pervade the cakes that go in next.

Remember that in a gas oven the greatest heat is at the bottom. Therefore when a cool oven is required the top shelf is the proper one to use.

Gas for cooking is not expensive if wisely used, but a careless cook can waste a great deal and cause an alarmingly large bill at the end of the quarter. The following hints make for economy:

See that all saucepans and kettles are scrupulously clean *outside*, as well as in. If the heat has to penetrate a layer of soot, more will be needed to cook the food.

Turn out the gas *before* removing the saucepan or kettle.

Never leave gas burning even for a minute when not in use. An extra match for relighting is cheaper than the wasted gas.

All heat which extends beyond the bottom of a cooking utensil and comes up the sides, is wasted. Never, for instance, use a large burner for a small kettle.

When food has come to the boil, and requires only to be left simmering, turn the burner half down.

When baking cakes or puddings in the oven, remember that sufficient heat is left to cook them for a little time after the gas is turned out. This means that you can extinguish your gas five or ten minutes before the food is fully baked.

When the oven is heated, seize the opportunity to bake as many things as possible; if you have still room to spare, put in a large pan of water to heat for toilet or domestic purposes.

A steamer with several compartments saves a lot of gas, since a whole dinner can often be cooked, one thing above another, over a single gas-jet (see page 63).

OIL STOVES.

A well-managed oil stove will do wonders, considering its size and cheapness. I have known the entire meals for a family of seven or eight to be cooked on the useful make known as the Primus, to give only one instance. The remarks made on page 48 regarding the use of the best oil for lamps, apply equally to stoves.

An oil stove should stand on a tin tray or square of oilcloth (which can be easily cleaned if food boils over) out of a draught. Keep the stove well filled, for if the oil burns out the wick will get charred and uneven. Wipe off grease at once while the stove is hot, and keep all parts absolutely clean, as already recommended in the case of a gas cooker. It may be washed occasionally in hot soda water and the black parts blackleaded.

Turn the wick low before putting out the stove, and do not turn it up again until after re-lighting.

SPIRIT STOVES.

Little stoves fed by methylated spirits are of various patterns and in war-time cost about 1/3 each. Those with wicks are somewhat safer, but decidedly slower than, the kind in which the spirit is poured into a circular pan. Great care must be taken to stand a spirit stove steadily in a safe place, as, being light, it is easily overturned.

It should never be placed in a draught, which blows the flame about and wastes it.

Though a spirit stove is equal only to simple cookery, it is a mistake to suppose that it is capable of nothing more than boiling a kettle. I have stewed fruit, made soup, poached and boiled eggs, fried rissoles and tomatoes on a small stove of the wick variety with complete success, and, given time, it will heat an iron satisfactorily.

Some of the wick stoves have a little screw which regulates the strength and size of the flame. In this case a lower heat may be obtained when boiling point is reached and only simmering is required.

If the methylated spirit gives out in the middle of cooking, it is essential to extinguish the flame before replenishing the reservoir. *It is most dangerous to pour in more spirit while the stove is alight.* It is liable to explode, causing severe or fatal injuries. Nor must a spirit stove be blown out. Always use the extinguisher belonging to it.

HAYBOX COOKERY.

A method of cooking which has much to recommend it is haybox cookery, which is daily gaining in favour, especially during the hot months of the year. It is economical, because it saves a great deal of gas, coal or oil; convenient, as removing the necessity of standing over a hot fire and watching food; satisfactory, inasmuch as foods requiring long, slow cooking get this better in a haybox than by any other method.

The principle underlying this form of cookery is very simple. The haybox is a padded box, filled with hay closely packed, into which saucepans of boiling food or liquid are put. Hay is a generator of heat and consequently will keep the contents of the saucepans for some hours at the same heat as they were when placed in the box. Soup, for instance, goes on boiling and consequently cooking, quite as satisfactorily as it would on the fire, but at a slower rate.

A haybox may be simple and quickly made at home at small expense; a bachelor girl will not need a large cooker. Buy for a few pence from the grocer a wooden butter-box or old packing case. Line the box neatly, first with sheets of brown paper and afterwards with felt, which can be nailed in place. The lid must also be lined, and if it is separate from the box, the two must be hinged together with leather hinges (or strong double strips cut from old Nappa kid gloves will do).

Upon the size of the haybox depends whether one or more saucepans will be used. Put the pan or pans into the box (already lined with a three-inch layer of hay at the bottom) and pack them tightly all round with hay, twisting and pressing it into shape so that the hole will remain when the saucepan is taken out. To fit over and keep the top of the plan warm, make a three-inch thick cushion of hay enclosed in a woollen cover that exactly fits the box. To fasten the lid down securely when cooking is in progress, fit the hay-box with a hasp and staple.

All food cooked in the box must first be started and got thoroughly hot on an ordinary coal, gas or oil stove; then, if transferred very quickly to the box while still on the boil, packed round tightly with hay and left for from one to six hours, it will be found beautifully cooked without the slightest attention having been given to it. Food cooked in this way takes quite twice as long as when done all through by fire. A haybox will not bake, fry or roast, but it will boil, steam and simmer to perfection. It saves an enormous amount of both fuel and trouble, and allows of food being prepared long beforehand.

Having started your Sunday dinner on the gas, for example, and then transferred it to the box, you may go out at ten, in the certainty of finding your meal cooked to a turn and piping hot, on your return at one or two o'clock.

Oatmeal porridge may be set in the haybox overnight; in the morning all it requires is five minutes on the fire to heat it up thoroughly. Stewed fruit needs only five to ten minutes cooking over a flame, and afterwards an hour in the haybox cooker; rice, sago, macaroni, tapioca and vermicelli about the same; potatoes and carrots, five minutes on the fire and one and a half hours in the haybox. From these instances you will be able to judge others, giving, if doubtful, rather more time in the hay than seems necessary.

Fortunately food very rarely takes any harm if left too long in a haybox, and for this reason the cooker is most convenient for girls working overtime, and uncertain when they will be home for their evening meals.

If the pans are not wanted for food, it is often convenient to keep water hot for washing in the morning, when time is scarce.

The Convenience of a Vacuum Flask.

Mention of keeping water hot is a reminder of the great convenience a thermos or vacuum flask may be to a bachelor girl, whether or not she possesses a haybox, and more especially if she has no gas ring or stove. A good half-pint flask may be bought for 4/- or 5/-, and will last for years. It will keep liquids poured in at boiling point at the same temperature for many hours—say seven or eight. After that period, the contents begin to cool very slowly.

If you want an early cup of tea in the morning, pour boiling water into your flask before going to bed and cork and screw it firmly. Next morning it will be just off the boil, and requires only a minute or two on the spirit stove before tea can be made.

After ten hours in a vacuum flask water will be hot enough for washing or washing up, and milk for drinking. A girl who knows she will come in tired and cold on a winter's night, with her evening meal to get, should leave hot milk in her flask in the morning, to warm and refresh her as soon as she gets in.

Anyone taking her own midday meal with her to work, especially if she is an outdoor toiler, will find a vacuum flask invaluable for supplying her with a hot drink or a hot cup of tea during the day, without equipment or bother.

If a flask is to be kept clean and sweet, one or two precautions must be observed. Firstly, always leave the cork out while the flask is not in use; if corked, it will soon smell musty.

After the flask has contained milk, wash it out as soon as possible in hot water containing a little soda. Remember that the cork must be washed also, or the deposit of milk upon it will turn sour.

Some people, when carrying tea in a flask, put it in ready milked and sugared for drinking, and the result is usually an unpleasant, musty taste. Sugar the tea, if you like, but do not add the milk. If you carry it separately in a small bottle and add it after pouring out, the tea will be delicious.

The power of the vacuum flask to keep liquids hot depends upon two essential points; first, the liquid when poured in must be actually boiling and must be corked down at once. Secondly, the flask must be absolutely filled, or the air which takes up the remainder of the space will rapidly cool the contents.

JAM JAR COOKERY.

If you are so placed that you have no gas or oil stove for cooking, and have to make the best of a tiny gas ring or an ordinary open fire, you will find jam jar cookery a tremendous boon. Anything that can be steamed may be cooked to perfection in a jam jar placed in a saucepan of boiling water.

Beg or buy one or two empty stoneware jam jars of different sizes, and with the addition of a saucepan your equipment is complete. By using a large saucepan and two or three small jars, it is possible to cook several things at the same time over a single gas jet. Jars fit better into an oval than a round pan.

Fill the saucepan with a few inches of water and let this heat while the food is being prepared. If, say, a cabbage is to be cooked, shred the vegetable into a jam jar, put this in the saucepan, when the water is boiling, tie greased paper over the top of the jar and steam till cooked. While the cabbage is cooking in the jar, a few small potatoes or a little rice may be boiling in the water, if you do not put in enough to impede the circulation of the liquid in the pan. Another jar in the same pan may contain a little steamed pudding, or a stew to eat with the cabbage.

Vegetables of many kinds, fruit, steamed puddings, fish, cutlets and oatmeal, may all be cooked to perfection in a jam jar. The boiling water, if not wanted for other purposes, is always useful for washing up or filling a hot bottle. Hot plates may be managed by removing the lid from the saucepan a few minutes before the cooking is finished. If the plates are put in its place, they will get nicely warmed.

The Advantages of a Steamer.

Jam jar cookery is really a simple substitute for the regular steamer, which, however, I have not included in the list of kitchen utensils (see page 41), as it is somewhat costly for the average bachelor girl. If the money can be spared it is well worth buying, as it saves a great deal of fuel.

A steamer has three or four compartments, one above another. The lowest holds water, which, when brought to the boil on a gas ring or stove, cooks the food in the various compartments above. In this way, in a four-tiered steamer, a complete dinner of meat, two vegetables and pudding may be cooked over a single flame. As in the case of jam jar cookery, the water compartment may be utilised to boil potatoes.

Steaming is a far better method of cooking than boiling, as it allows none of the goodness of the food to escape in steam. The use of the steamer also saves the time and bother spent in washing three or four separate saucepans. Steamers cost from 4/6 upwards.

PORTABLE LUNCHES.

Numerous girl workers, as, for instance, teachers in rural schools who live too far away to go home in the midday interval, must perforce take their lunch with them and eat it at work; and many business girls would be far wiser to follow the same plan, rather than spend an inadequate daily sum on inadequate food at a restaurant. At present prices ninepence goes only a little way at a teashop, but that sum spent daily on a home-made lunch will give a meal full of nourishment and variety.

As work can only be well done on nutritious food, the basis of the meal must contain protein, which can be given in the form of meat, eggs or cheese, sometimes one and sometimes another. Other necessary components are starch (secured by including bread or potatoes), fat (milk, butter, cream, suet), sugar (cakes, biscuits or chocolate), and fruit. Many foods, of course, are ruled out because they will not carry well, and the lunch must also be made up of quickly prepared edibles, since the bachelor girl is far too hurried in the morning to spend much time in concocting her midday meal.

The following specimen menus for a week give an idea of the variety that may be obtained:

MONDAY.—Cold sausage sandwiches, a slice of Madeira cake and an apple.

TUESDAY.—Sandwiches of cheese biscuits spread with meat or fish paste, two small rock cakes and a banana.

WEDNESDAY.—A large meat turnover or sausage roll, a few sweet biscuits and an orange.

THURSDAY.—Sardine sandwiches, a Bath bun, a tartlet and two small pears.

FRIDAY.—Slices of thin brown bread and butter, a hard-boiled egg, a little lettuce or cucumber, a slice of seed cake and a handful of cherries or a few figs according to the season.

SATURDAY.—Two buttered rolls with slices of ham between their halves, a bar of chocolate, a piece of shortbread and a tomato (or in summer, no shortbread or tomato, but strawberries and cream).

These suggestions do not by any means exhaust the possibilities, of which there are so many that put-up lunches need never grow monotonous.

As regards beverages, the possessor of a vacuum flask (see page 61) can carry in it tea, coffee, cocoa, Oxo, Ivelcon or hot milk in cold weather, and lemonade or cold milk during the summer. The only objection to this plan, if much walking has to be done, is that a full flask adds considerably to the weight of the lunch. Sometimes water is obtainable on the spot (a spoonful of lemonade powder can always be added), or there is a gas ring on which a kettle can be boiled.

Tea should not be drunk with meat lunches, as the tannin in it acts injuriously on the digesting of meat.

Nothing keeps food quite so fresh as a tin receptacle of some sort, but failing this the meal may be carried in a covered basket or one of those light woven rush bags costing about sixpence or ninepence.

Sandwiches should be wrapped in a clean old serviette or in grease-proof paper, while cakes and fruit should have separate paper bags. A lettuce keeps freshest if enveloped in a slightly damp cloth. Cream should be bought on the spot, or conveyed in the little cardboard pail in which it is sold. This must be kept upright all the time.

It is well to remember that if a menu contains cream, or if the beverage selected is milk, less solid food will be required for the rest of the meal, as both milk and cream are exceedingly nourishing. Milk should not be drunk at lunch by those who are liable to constipation, as it aggravates the complaint.

There is more convenience in eating a portable lunch if a cup and saucer (or glass), plate, spoon and knife are kept at the place where lunch is consumed.

RECIPES

In this section are given a few recipes carefully chosen with the limitations and needs of the bachelor girl in mind. They will be found useful for making a start, but after a short experience in cooking them you should go on to the wider scope afforded by a good cheap cookery book, so that your catering may not become monotonous.

How to Make Tea.

Fill a kettle with fresh cold water from the tap. Do not use water from the hot tap, or water which has been heating over the fire for some time, if you wish to make really nice tea. As soon as the water boils (*not* five or ten or thirty minutes afterwards) it must be used. While it is boiling, warm the teapot, either by standing it on or near the stove, or by pouring a little hot water into it from the kettle, rinsing it round and emptying away the water.

When the kettle boils, put the tea into the pot, and pour the boiling water over it. The amount of tea used should be a teaspoonful per person, if there are two or three people, or about a teaspoonful and a half for one person. Over three, the quantities per head gradually lessen.

After pouring in the boiling water, put the lid on the teapot and stand it in a warm place to infuse for from three to five minutes, when it will be ready to pour out.

The cardinal points of good tea-making are:
1. Fresh water freshly boiled, and used as soon as it boils.
2. A nicely heated teapot.
3. Tea poured out before it has "drawn" long enough to get in the least bitter.

How to Make Coffee.

Coffee is rather more trouble than tea, but it is well to have it at breakfast-time, as otherwise rather too much tea may be drunk, with consequent injury to the digestion. To make the very best coffee, you must roast and grind your own beans, but this is rarely possible for the bachelor girl, and as a good substitute she must buy ground coffee of good quality, *without any chicory in it.*

Boil half a pint of water in a saucepan, and as soon as it boils measure two teaspoonfuls of coffee into an enamel mug or other vessel and pour the boiling water in. (Enamel is preferable to china, as it retains the heat longer.) Cover the vessel (a saucer will do for this) and set it in a hot place for seven minutes.

Meanwhile heat half a pint of milk. It is better that it should not actually boil, but it must be made thoroughly hot. There is less risk of milk burning if it is heated in an enamel saucepan. As the milk will take only three or four minutes to heat, do not start it immediately you have covered the coffee, or it will be ready too soon and will get cool.

At the end of the seven minutes pour the coffee through a strainer into the coffee pot, which should be already warmed. Pour the milk into a jug, also warmed, and serve. The correct proportions with coffee of this strength are coffee and milk in equal parts.

The cardinal points in good coffee-making are:
1. Unadulterated coffee.
2. The water must be used as soon as it boils.
3. Use plenty of coffee and let it stand the full seven minutes.
4. Use every precaution to serve the coffee piping hot.

How to Make Cocoa.

Cocoa may be made in three ways.
1. With water, in which case a little cold milk is added at table, as with tea.
2. With water and milk in equal proportions.
3. With milk entirely.

The last method is the nicest and most expensive. The second is perhaps the most generally used, and is more easily digested than all-milk cocoa, so I will describe this method in detail.

The quantity of cocoa to be used depends on

the brand selected, and you should follow the directions on the packet or tin in this respect. Measure the correct quantity into a cup, and mix it smoothly to a paste with a very little cold milk. It is important that there should be no lumps and that the mixing should be thorough.

Put a teacupful each of cold water and milk into the same saucepan and bring them to the boil. Then pour them over the cocoa paste in the cup, and stir well, when the cocoa is ready to drink.

If you are making water cocoa, the paste may be made either with milk or water, and boiling water is poured over. For all-milk cocoa, put milk only into the saucepan.

Sausage Toast.

Required:—2 sausages, a large, thick slice of bread, a little dripping and flour.

Put the slice of bread in the oven or near the stove to get warm. Fry the sausages in fat until they are nicely brown, and arrange them neatly on the bread. Dredge a little flour into the frying-pan and pour in enough boiling water to make a nice gravy. Stir over the fire until it thickens, then pour over the bread. Quantities enough for one.

Fried Sausages with Chip Potatoes.

Required:—2 sausages, 3 or 4 large potatoes, $1\frac{1}{2}$ ozs. of clarified fat, salt and pepper.

Wash and peel the potatoes, cutting them into

slices a quarter of an inch thick; then cut again into small, thin sticks.

Melt the fat in a frying-pan. When quite hot (a blue smoke will arise) prick the sausages with a fork and put them into the fat. Fry till brown. Then take them out, heat the fat till very hot, put in the potatoes and fry a golden brown. Drain them on kitchen paper laid on a colander. Arrange the potatoes round the sausages on a hot dish and serve at once. Quantities enough for two.

HAM CROQUETTES.

Required:—$\frac{1}{2}$ lb. of cooked ham (can be bought ready-cooked), $\frac{1}{4}$ lb. of cold cooked potatoes, 1 hard-boiled egg, yolk of another egg and 1 tablespoonful of minced parsley.

Chop the ham and hard-boiled egg with a knife on a pastry board. Mix them with the parsley. Then add the potatoes, pepper and salt to taste, and finally moisten the mixture with the yolk of egg. Flour your hands, and in them roll portions of the mixture into balls, which fry a nice brown in boiling fat. Quantities enough for two.

LEFT-OVER SAUSAGES.

(A recipe for using up small quantities of left-over meat and vegetables.)

Required:—3 tablespoonfuls of minced or chopped vegetables (any kind, cooked), 1 tablespoonful of minced cold meat, 1 tablespoonful of breadcrumbs and 1 egg.

Mix well together the vegetables, meat and breadcrumbs. Beat the egg, and mix it in to bind the mixture together. Roll into a sausage shape, dip in breadcrumbs and fry brown in boiling fat. Quantities enough for two.

STEWED TRIPE.

In war-time tripe is one of the cheapest meat dishes.

Required:—¾ lb. of tripe, ½ pt. of milk, 4 onions, seasonings.

Tripe is partly cooked when bought, so does not require stewing as long as most meats. Slice the onions, and put them into a stewpan or saucepan with the tripe and milk (or half milk and half water). Cover the pot and cook slowly for an hour. If only half milk is used, the liquid should be thickened with a small teaspoonful of corn-flour. Quantities enough for two.

PORRIDGE.

Required:—2 tablespoonfuls of fine oatmeal, ½ pt. boiling water, a pinch of salt.

A double saucepan is needed for making porridge. Half fill the outer saucepan with boiling water, and put half a pint of boiling water into the inner one with a small saltspoonful of salt. When it boils gradually sprinkle in the oatmeal, stirring well all the time with a wooden spoon. When quite smooth, boil for thirty minutes, stirring occasionally.

FRIED PORRIDGE CAKES.

Required:—1 tablespoonful (or more) of cold porridge, flour, 1 teaspoonful of chopped parsley, tomato ketchup.

This lunch or supper dish is an excellent way of using left-over porridge. Knead it with enough flour to make a pliable paste, mix in the parsley, and shape into two small flat cakes. Fry golden-brown in fat, and serve on a hot plate with prepared tomato sauce or ketchup poured over.

For a sweet dish, omit the parsley, and serve with a little butter, and golden syrup or jam. Quantities enough for one.

BUTTERED EGGS.

Required:—2 eggs, 1½ ozs. of butter or margarine, 2 slices of bread, 2 tablespoonfuls of milk, salt and pepper.

Toast the bread and cut away the crust. Break the eggs into a basin, and beat them well. Season with pepper and salt, add the milk and mix thoroughly. Melt the butter or margarine in a saucepan, add the egg mixture, and stir very quickly with a wooden spoon over the fire to a thick, creamy consistency. Pour over the toast and serve at once. Be careful that the eggs do not cook more than a minute or two. Quantities enough for two.

POACHED EGGS.

Required:—1 or 2 eggs, toasted bread and butter.

Toast and butter hot a large slice of bread and cut away the crust. Half fill a frying-pan with water, add a teaspoonful of salt, and let the water boil. Then break in the eggs separately and as neatly as possible, and let them cook two or three minutes until set. Place the eggs on the toast and serve. Quantities enough for one.

CHEESE BALLS.

Required:—1 large egg, grated cheese, breadcrumbs.

Beat the egg slightly and mix into it enough breadcrumbs and grated cheese (equal quantities of each) to make a firm paste. Divide this in half and roll each portion into a ball. Dip the balls in breadcrumbs until well covered and fry golden-brown in lard or dripping. Stale cheese grates best and is more economical. Quantities enough for one.

WELSH RAREBIT.

Required:—Cheese (2 ozs.), 1 round of buttered toast, $\frac{1}{2}$ oz. of butter, a little stock or milk, and seasonings.

Melt the butter in an enamelled saucepan. Grate the cheese, and season with pepper, salt and mustard. Stir in enough white stock or milk to make the mixture the consistency of thick cream. Stir over the fire till the cheese has dissolved, then spread on the toast, dust lightly, with cayenne and eat at once. Quantities enough for two.

CHEESE CIRCLETS.

Required:—Cheese, bread, butter and seasonings.

Slice some fairly stale bread into half inch thicknesses, and stamp into rounds with a pastry cutter. Butter both sides very thinly and toast lightly. Grate the cheese and season to taste with pepper and salt. Heap on each hot round a pile of the mixture and place under the grill for a minute to melt the cheese.

Cheese Fritters.

Required:—2 ozs. of grated cheese, 2 tablespoonfuls of flour, 1 dessertspoonful of mustard, $\frac{1}{2}$ gill of milk, 2 whites of eggs, pepper and salt.

Mix together the cheese flour, mustard, seasonings and milk. Slightly beat the whites of eggs, add them to the mixture and form it into fritters, which fry in lard to a delicate golden-brown. Quantities enough for two.

Fish Cream.

Required:—1 fillet of sole, 1 tablespoonful of cream, lemon juice, pepper and salt.

Wash the fish and shred it finely. Season it and steam by placing between two greased plates over a saucepan of fast-boiling water. When cooked, mix in the cream and flavour with a few drops of lemon juice. Serve very hot in a ring of mashed potatoes or rice boiled in water. Quantities enough for one.

Stewed Whiting.

Required:—1 whiting (skinned), lemon juice and seasoning.

Wash, dry and season the fish. Put its tail into its mouth, and fasten with a skewer. Steam between two greased plates over a saucepan of boiling water for thirty to forty minutes. Serve with a little lemon juice squeezed over. Quantities enough for one.

Lemon Sole and Tomato.

Required:—1 lemon sole, 1 small Spanish onion, ½ oz. of butter, a little flour, a few drops of anchovy essence, 1 large tomato, 2 tablespoonfuls of milk and seasoning.

Slice the onion and tomato in rings, and lay the fish in a shallow baking-dish with these and a few tiny lumps of butter. Make some small cuts in the flesh and put a drop of anchovy in each. Dredge lightly with flour, put more butter on the top, and pour the milk over all. Bake for twenty-five minutes in a hot oven, and serve in the baking-dish. Quantities enough for one.

Fish Cakes.

Required:—¼ lb. of cooked potatoes (or rather more), ¼ lb. of cooked fish, I small egg, salt and pepper.

Remove all bones and skin from the fish, and mix it well with the potatoes (mashed). Beat the egg well, and add half of it to the mixture, seasoning to taste. Work all to a smooth firm paste, and form into balls. Flatten the balls into cakes, and brush them over with the other half of the egg. Roll them in breadcrumbs, and fry golden-brown. Drain on kitchen paper before serving. Quantities enough for one.

Mushrooms on Toast.

Required:—¼ lb. of mushrooms, 1 oz. of butter, 1 tablespoonful of brown or tomato sauce, the yolk of 1 egg, lemon juice, seasonings and triangles of buttered toast.

Trim the mushrooms and chop them rather large. Cook them very slowly for ten minutes in a saucepan, together with the butter, salt, pepper and lemon juice. Stir in the yolk of egg and sauce, and let the mixture heat again. Pile it on the toast and garnish with parsley or slices of lemon. Quantities enough for two.

SALMON IN SALAD.

(A very nice hot-weather supper dish.)

Required:—½ tin of salmon, a small lettuce, 2 large or 3 small tomatoes, a few slices of cucumber, and (if liked) a hard-boiled egg.

Divide the salmon into suitable small pieces. Tear the lettuce small between the fingers, slice the cucumber and tomatoes, remove the egg from the shell and cut into slices. Arrange all the ingredients effectively in a salad bowl or glass dish. Pour over them a plain salad dressing, or serve a bought salad cream separately. Quantities enough for two. Sardines are delicious served in the same way.

VEGETABLES AND SALADS.

BOILED POTATOES.

Required:—Potatoes, salt.

Choose potatoes as far as possible of the same size. Wash them, peel them as thinly as possible and put them in a pan of cold water if they are not to be cooked immediately. To cook, put the potatoes into a saucepan, cover them with cold, salted water, and bring to the boil; then simmer rapidly for twenty to thirty minutes. Drain well, return the saucepan to the fire, sprinkle the potatoes with salt and shake until they are floury.

New Potatoes (Boiled).

Required:—New potatoes, salt.

Scrape the potatoes with a knife. Put them into a saucepan containing sufficient boiling water to cover them, and add salt to taste when partly cooked. They will be ready for the table after twenty minutes' cooking.

Boiled Spanish Onions.

Required:—4 medium-sized onions, melted butter and salt.

Peel the onions and boil them gently for five minutes in salted water. Drain on a sieve and then throw them into a saucepan of cold water. Simmer until tender right through but not until they begin to break. Serve on a hot dish, with melted butter poured over them. Quantities enough for two.

Steamed Green Peas.

(An instance of Jam Jar Cookery.)

Required:—Peas, 2 ozs. of butter, 2 sprigs of mint, $\frac{1}{2}$ teaspoonful of salt and $\frac{1}{2}$ teaspoonful of castor sugar.

Shell the peas, and put them into a large stone jam jar with the butter, salt, sugar and mint. Cover the jar closely and stand it in a large saucepan of boiling water. Cook till the peas are tender, remove the mint and serve.

Cauliflower with Tomato Sauce.

Required:—1 small cauliflower, ½ cupful of tomato sauce, butter, a pinch of salt and one of sugar.

Boil the cauliflower in salted water and drain it well. Place in a hot vegetable dish and strain over it half a cupful of tomato sauce, seasoned with a tiny lump of butter, sugar and salt. Quantities enough for two.

Winter Potato Salad.

Required:—4 or 5 cold boiled potatoes, tomato sauce, a few capers and seasonings.

Slice the potatoes and lay them in a salad bowl or glass dish. Pour over them here and there little dabs of tomato sauce and sprinkle with a few capers. Serve with a ready-prepared dressing, or mix one with oil, vinegar, salt and pepper. Quantities enough for two.

Summer Potato Salad.

Required:—4 or 5 cold boiled potatoes, half a small cucumber, 1 large and one small tomato, and salad dressing.

Scoop out all the pulp and juice from the large tomato. Mash the potatoes and beat into them thoroughly the tomato juice and pulp. Slice the cucumber, chop the slices small and add them to the salad. Pile in the centre of a glass dish, and make a border round of additional slices of cucumber. Garnish the centre pile with the small tomato cut into neat sections. Serve with dressing. Quantities enough for two.

Lettuce and Cucumber Salad.

Required:—1 small lettuce, a penny bunch of mustard and cress, ½ small cucumber, dressing.

Wash the lettuce, remove the outer leaves and tear the remainder small with the fingers. Add the mustard and cress and the cucumber (sliced), and mix all thoroughly together. Just before serving add gradually, mixing each time before putting in more, a simple dressing. Quantities enough for two.

Some Simple Puddings.

Such things as custard, jellies, blancmange and junket may be made by following the directions which accompany the packets. Jellies are always improved if a few slices of banana are placed at the bottom of the mould before the jelly is poured in, and they are more nourishing when served with a little cream. Junket, custard and blancmange are all a nice addition to stewed fruit; and blancmange is also excellent served with jam.

How to Stew Fruit.

Prepare the fruit in whatever way may be necessary. Currants and gooseberries must be topped and tailed, apples and pears peeled and sliced, rhubarb cut into short pieces, &c.

Put the fruit into a stewpan or saucepan, and well cover it with cold water. Add several spoonfuls of brown sugar and bring to the boil. Then simmer at a lower heat until the fruit is quite tender, and pour into a dish to cool.

Sponge Cake Pudding.

Required:—4 penny sponge cakes, ½ pt. of custard, jam.

This is one of the easiest of all puddings to make, and may be served either hot or cold. Slice the sponge cakes in halves, and spread each half with jam; then arrange them in a glass dish. Make the custard and pour it over the cakes, serving either hot or cold. In the fruit season a layer of crushed strawberries or raspberries may be used instead of jam. Quantities enough for two.

Jam Fritters.

Required:—Slices of bread, butter and jam.

Cut slices of bread fairly thick, and trim them into squares of about two inches. Butter them thinly on each side, and fry them a golden colour in a little lard. Put a dab of red jam on each square and serve very hot.

Apricot Fritters

are made in the same way, but the squares must be rather larger, and half an apricot, with its hollow filled with a tiny dab of whipped cream, is laid on each instead of jam.

HOUSEHOLD DUTIES

Many bachelor girls "do" entirely for themselves, which is certainly the cheapest way; others employ a charwoman for an hour or two a day, and need to have a practical knowledge of her duties—how and when they should be done—if they wish the household wheels to run efficiently. Cooking is dealt with elsewhere in this book; here I propose to talk about housework, of which I am assuming the bachelor girl has no knowledge at all.

A girl "doing" for herself in a bed-sitting room has least work to get through, as she has only one room to look after. In the morning, apart from the cooking and laying of breakfast, there will be the room to tidy, the bed to make, the dirty water to be poured away and replaced by fresh; also boots or shoes to clean, and the breakfast things to wash up and put away.

If an early start has to be made, and time is scarce in the morning, the work should be lightened as much as possible by a little forethought. The breakfast table may be set overnight and protected from dust by being covered with a clean cloth, while the china can be stacked in a basin of hot water after the meal and left to be properly washed up at midday or in the evening. If a coal fire is used, this should, if the weather is not too cold, be allowed to die out shortly before bedtime and relaid overnight ready for the morning. If this is out of the question, never rely on cooking breakfast on a fire which has to be laid on getting up, or there will be much delay. Water can be boiling for tea or coffee on a spirit stove long before the fire gives out sufficient heat for the purpose.

When a girl lives alone, her room need not be swept and dusted every day, as one person brings in so little dirt. It is a good plan to dust and sweep one day and to clean two pairs of shoes the next; among other things, such a plan insures that the same footwear will not be worn two days running, and so economises leather.

If there are two rooms in question, one might be thoroughly tidied each day, the other being left.

When two girls live together, they will naturally share the daily work, dividing it up in the way best suited to their capabilities. A sensible arrangement in the morning is for one to cook and lay the breakfast, while the other tidies the rooms, gets fresh washstand water and so on. Each girl should make her own bed, or one might make both and the other clean the boots. Housework becomes less monotonous if jobs are changed over every week or month.

In a flat a charwoman will probably be employed, as there is a good deal of extra work, such as keeping the kitchen, bathroom and hall clean, and cleaning the front steps, if there are any. So much for the daily routine. Weekly or more occasional jobs include polishing the silver, sorting and entering clothes for the laundry, doing fine bits of washing at home, mending, Saturday shopping for the week-end, and putting up clean curtains from time to time. If accounts are run with the tradespeople, the books must be paid once a week.

Bed Making.

As soon as you get up in the morning, strip your bed by spreading all the bedclothes over a chair placed at the foot of the bed, and arching the mattress. Leave it to air while you are dressing and breakfasting. Remember that a room must never be dusted or swept while the bed is stripped, or the dust will get into the sheets and blankets.

To make the bed, begin by turning the mattress, so that the side which was downwards is placed uppermost. Lay the under-blanket and sheet smoothly in position on the mattress, tucking them in. If the bolster is not provided with a separate case, roll part of the sheet neatly round it and tuck in the ends. Shake up the bolster, and then shake the pillow before laying it on the bolster. Put on the upper sheet, leaving enough at the top to turn well over, and tuck in well at the sides and bottom. Put on and tuck in the blankets; turn them down below the pillow, with the sheet over them.

Put on the counterpane or bedspread neatly and evenly, and lastly the eiderdown, if there is one; or fold it up neatly at the foot of the bed. The nightwear should go either under the pillow or in a nightdress case laid outside the bed.

At night remove and fold up the bedspread, and lay the eiderdown over the bed.

Put a pair of clean sheets on the bed once a fortnight, with fresh bolster and pillow cases; or the bed may have one clean sheet every week, the clean one being used as the upper and the soiled one as the under sheet.

Washstand Work.

Empty all the dirty water into the slop pail, which must afterwards be rinsed out, preferably with hot water. Wash over all the toilet china with hot water and dry it on a cloth kept for this particular purpose. Rinse out the cloth after use, and hang it (if possible, in the open air) to dry. Fill the washstand jug and water bottle with fresh water from the tap. When the room is dusted remove all china from the washstand and dust it thoroughly, going over the marble top with a damp cloth.

Sweeping and Dusting a Room.

Remove the tablecloth and hearthrug and shake them outside. Take all small pieces of furniture out of the room, or pile them on the table or bed. Sprinkle the carpet with tea leaves saved from breakfast or the previous day, and sweep it with a stiff carpet brush or broom, taking up the pieces in a dustpan. Sweep the oilcloth or boards in the room with a soft broom, or go over the oilcloth with a damp cloth. Labour can be much lessened by using a carpet sweeper and an O-Cedar mop instead of brooms. Empty the contents of the dustpan on to the fire or in the dustbin.

Dust every piece of furniture thoroughly, removing ornaments from mantelpiece, dressing-table, &c., and dusting them before replacing them. Dressing-table covers and mantel borders should be shaken out of the window before they are put back. Pay particular attention to crevices, corners and rails of chairs, and if there is a bed in the room dust its rails and frame. The window ledges, mirrors, pictures and skirting board must also be dusted. Every few minutes during dusting shake the duster out of the window, to rid it of its accumulated dirt.

Replace all ornaments and small articles of furniture in their places, and bring back the hearthrug and tablecloth from outside the room.

Washing Up.

For tea or breakfast things that do not include any greasy plates or dishes, you will require only a single enamel basin half full of hot water, a mop and a teacloth.

Collect all crumbs and pieces from the plates and throw them away or burn them. Empty dregs of tea or coffee from the cups and pot; do not throw away tea leaves, but save them for sprinkling the carpet when sweeping. Then stack up the china in the bowl of hot water, and put in also the spoons and other silver.

Always wash silver or plate first. If a little mop, costing 3½d., is used for washing up, your hands will hardly get wet at all. Nothing spoils hands so much, making them rough and chapped, as having them continually in and out of greasy water.

Wipe the spoons over well with the mop until perfectly clean, and put them, bowls downwards, to drain. If you have no proper sink or draining board, as is probably the case, use a piece of white American cloth or a metal tray for the purpose.

Next wash the china in the same way with the mop, not forgetting to cleanse particularly well round the handles of cups, teapot and jugs. Put it to drain upside down, so that the water may run out of the interior.

Obstinate tea or coffee stains inside cups may be removed by rubbing a little coarse salt over the marks with your finger.

When all the china is washed, wash out the bowl with hot water (and a little soda, if necessary), and turn it upside down to drain.

Dry the silver with a clean teacloth, rubbing it up slightly at the same time. This rubbing saves much labour when polishing silver, if it is done regularly at every washing up.

Next dry all the china, taking particular care that the interior of jugs, teapots and coffee pots are quite dry, as damp gives them an unpleasant smell. If a tea or coffee pot is used only occasionally, it is a good plan to put it away with a lump of sugar inside. This sucks up the moisture, and keeps the inside dry.

Lastly, put the china and plate away in their proper places. Wash out the mop in hot water with a little soap, wring it as dry as possible, and hang it up to dry. If the washing up has been done in a sink, clear away and burn all pieces that may be lying about, and scrub round the sink with a special brush kept for the purpose, after sluicing it with clean water from the tap. Hang the teacloth up to dry. To keep it clean and sweet, it must be washed and boiled every few days.

Glasses should be washed first of all, before any silver or china. After washing them inside and out, in hot water, with the mop, rinse them by holding for a moment under the cold tap or by plunging them in a bowl of cold water. This prevents smearing and makes them bright and clear.

Knives should first be wiped over with a piece of paper, which must be burnt after use. The handles must never go into the water or they will come loose from the blades. For this reason the easiest way of washing knives is to stand them in a jug half full of hot water, so that the blades get wet, while the handles are above the water. Wipe the blades over with the mop, and if the handles are sticky go over them with a slightly damp cloth. For the cleaning of knives, see page 91.

Greasy plates and dishes should be washed last, so that they will not spoil the water for cleaner articles. Wipe off all bits and as much grease as possible from the plates with small squares of newspaper before putting them into the bowl. (A pile of cut paper squares should hang on a string in some handy corner, and be replenished from time to time.) The water in which greasy things are washed should contain a lump of washing soda and some soap powder. Some people use these cleansers for every sort of washing up, but it is not at all necessary in the case of tea things, and the soda in the water is bad for the hands.

If you have a plate rack over the sink, the clean plates and dishes can be put into it wet and left to dry. Failing this piece of scullery equipment, the plates must drain, bottom upwards, and then be dried in the usual way. Greasy china should never be left unwashed for hours after a meal, or the grease will harden and be much more difficult to remove. If it is more convenient to delay the proper washing up, plunge the plates in a basin of hot water containing soda and leave them there to soak.

Saucepans, frying-pans, tins, &c., must be cleansed after the china. Immediately after use each should have been filled with water, to prevent the grease from drying and hardening. Put each saucepan in the washing-up bowl, and thoroughly scour both inside and out with a saucepan brush, which costs about 6d. If burnt, clean by rubbing with fine ash or sand. Place wrong way up in a warm spot to dry. Soda is helpful in cleaning, but should be used very sparingly in the case of enamel ware.

Cleaning Knives.

It is not necessary to have a knife board, if economy must be studied in fitting up the kitchen. Instead of sprinkling a board with knife powder and then rubbing the blade along it, a knife can be made quite bright by rubbing it, first on one side and then on the other, with a cork dipped in knife powder. Keep the knife quite flat while it is being cleaned, or the edge may get blunted. After polishing, dust the knives and put them away.

Stains on the blades of knives can be removed with Brookes' soap, or by dipping a slice of raw potato into bathbrick and rubbing it on the steel. Afterwards polish as usual.

If the handles are stained, rub them with a damp cloth dipped in kitchen salt; or, failing this, use salt mixed to a paste with a little lemon juice and applied with a soft flannel. If the latter remedy has been used, rub the blades with dry flour afterwards, to remove all traces of the acid.

Cleaning Silver.

Silver or plated spoons and forks do not need much special attention if they are regularly rubbed when being dried, but every week or fortnight a time should be set aside for polishing them, together with all silver trinket boxes, photograph frames, candlesticks, thimbles, &c.

Various ready-to-use plate powders are sold, and save trouble; or a paste may be made at home of whiting mixed with water. If the metal is discoloured, use liquid ammonia or methylated spirits instead of water.

Rub the paste all over the article with a bit of cotton rag, and polish with a chamois leather until it shines very brightly. Some people finish rubbing paste over everything before starting to polish, but this is a mistake, for if the paste has time to dry on it is very difficult to remove from the crevices. It is far better to complete one article at a time. If there is any chased or embossed pattern, use a soft plate brush to get the paste out of the crevices.

Cleaning Boots and Shoes.

It is easy to spend several shillings on an elaborate outfit for boot cleaning, most of which is quite unnecessary. Everything required for both black and brown footwear may be bought for ninepence or less. You will need (for black shoes) a brush for applying the blacking, a tin of blacking or polish, and a black velvet polishing pad; for brown shoes, a rubber for applying the polish (or a second brush), a tin of brown cream and a brown velvet polishing pad. By having the equipment for each kind of footwear the same colour as the shoes for which it is intended, you run no risk of inadvertently using the black brush for brown shoes, or vice versa. You will also need a tiny sponge and a bit of pointed firewood for use when boots are very muddy. The velvet pads can be made at home of old bits of velvet stuffed with rags, or bought at a Penny Bazaar, as can the brown rubber.

Girls living in the country and doing much walking over bad roads, often get their boots wet through and caked with mud. In this case, the boots should be left in a warm room (but not near a fire) to dry. It may be as long as twenty-four hours, in winter, before they are ready to be cleaned.

Scrape off as much mud as possible by gentle use of the pointed stick. A knife must never be employed, as sooner or later it is sure to slip and cut the leather. Dip the little sponge in water, wring it nearly dry, and wipe over the boots with it, to remove the last traces of mud. It is ruin to footwear to put on polish *over* mud.

Dip the brush into the blacking and rub it all over the boot, not forgetting the heel. Then polish vigorously with the velvet pad until a good shine appears all over.

Boots which are not muddy do not need the stick and sponge treatment, but can have the blacking or cream applied straight away. If boots are very dusty, as often happens in summer, begin by wiping them over with a duster.

An economical substitute for brown boot cream is the inside of a banana skin, rubbed all over the leather and then polished.

Boots and shoes keep their shape much better if they are put on trees as soon as they are taken off the feet. Failing trees, the toes may be well stuffed with soft paper.

For the cleaning of white shoes, see page 104.

Laying and Lighting a Fire.

Remove the hearthrug and spread a cloth or newspapers in front of the fireplace to protect the carpet. Put on the cloth the fender and fireirons, and all laying and lighting materials, such as paper, wood, coal, matches, hearthbrush and dustpan.

Take out all the cinders from the grate and from underneath, laying the cinders on one side, and sweeping all the ash into the dustpan. If there is a firebrick in the fireplace, put it in position at the back of the grate.

Take two or three double sheets of newspaper, crumple them loosely into balls, and put them at the bottom of the grate. Lay over them a number of pieces of wood in criss-cross layers, and on the wood put a layer of rather small pieces of coal mixed with cinders. Finally put on a few larger-sized pieces of coal, replace the fender and fireirons, take up the cloth and put down the hearthrug.

Pull out the front under the fireplace, to cause a good draught, and light the fire by holding a match to the paper in two or three places. When the wood and coal have caught nicely, add a little more coal, if necessary, and push in the bottom, or the fire will burn away too fast, wasting fuel.

It is both dangerous and extravagant to get a fire to go by using candle ends or paraffin. If a fire will not burn, it is probably because the wood is damp, or too little paper or wood was used. There is a decided knack in laying a fire, which some people only acquire after a good deal of practice.

After a fire is lighted, sweep the hearth perfectly clean. Put the dust into the dustbin, and save the cinders for use when a slow fire is needed.

THE DRESS ALLOWANCE

Having decided how much you can afford to spend on dress (see page 10), you must keep rigidly within this amount and not be tempted to go even a little beyond it. It is best to draw your dress allowance quarterly, as far more can be done with a substantial sum four times a year than with a trifling one every week or month. The allowance should not be divided exactly into four, but should be arranged so that the biggest sums fall due at the most expensive times of year.

Let us suppose that you are a girl with £15 a year to spend on dress, and that you do not wear uniform, but the ordinary clothes required by a school teacher or office worker. The most expensive time in the whole year is undoubtedly the autumn quarter, when you have to buy new winter clothes; next comes spring, which costs you less, because a summer outfit is cheaper than a winter one. You will not spend as much in either the summer or winter quarters.

Try dividing your money in this way: September, £4 10s. 0d.; December, £3 10s. 0d.; March, £4; June, £3: total, £15 per annum.

Out of this sum you will have to provide yourself with boots and shoes, summer and winter underwear, corsets, a neat coat and skirt, a full length winter coat, blouses, hats, a couple of cotton frocks for summer, and a nice house gown for winter. Evening dress need not be considered in war-time, but you will need a waterproof, a sports coat and oddments in the way of gloves, ribbons and veils.

Of course the complete list will not be bought new every year, as many of the items will last two years or more. One year perhaps you will get winter underwear, a waterproof and cotton frocks; the next, a winter coat and an afternoon dress. If you wear your costume all the time you will need a new one every year, preferably in the spring, but with a winter coat and cotton summer frocks to save it, it ought to last for eighteen months or two years.

A good deal less will be spent if a girl makes at any rate some of her blouses, cotton frocks and underwear, and trims her everyday hats. Here is an actual year's budget, taken from the account book of a girl who spends £15 per annum on her clothes, and divides her money quarterly in the way I have suggested.

Blouses	...	...	...	...	£2 7	6
Skirts	...	...	...	...	1 14	0
Hats	...	...	...	...	1 3	9½
Sports Coat		...	...	...	12	11
Shoes and Spats		...	...	...	1 11	4½
Stockings (7 pairs)			...	...	11	8¼
Underwear (including Lingerie Ribbons)					1 11	4
		Carried forward		...	£9 12	7½

Brought forward	...		£9	12	$7\frac{1}{2}$
Corsets	...	...	...	...	1	9	0
Material for two Frocks	...	...		19	5
Summer Dressing Gown	...	...		4	$6\frac{3}{4}$
Gloves (5 pairs, various)	...	...		10	$9\frac{3}{4}$
Cleaning	...	...	...	...		3	9
Miscellaneous—Shoe repairs, Collars,					
Buttons, Veils, Ribbons, etc.	...		1	19	$9\frac{1}{2}$
			£15	0	0

This budget is for the year beginning June 1st, 1915, and ending May 31st, 1916, so that it deals with war prices; these were especially noticed in the buying of woollen underwear, stockings, shoes and the two skirts, one of tweed and the other of navy serge. Other prices were not noticeably higher than in pre-war days.

During the year in question, the girl whose budget I have quoted had in hand a costume and winter coat, so was spared the cost of these two heavy items; on the other hand, she bought two woollen skirts at a considerable increase over the usual price, a sports coat, winter combinations of pure wool, a new corset (an item on which she is particularly extravagant), and an unusually expensive blouse. Of the six blouses got for £2 7s. 6d., three were bought ready-made and the other three made up at home; a little underwear and two frocks, one a cotton, the other a winter house frock, were also the result of home dress-making. The £1 9s. 0d. allotted for corsets included a new pair, made to measure, at 25/- and the repairing of an old pair. The £1 11s. $4\frac{1}{4}$ d.

for shoes (this girl does not wear boots) included two pairs of walking shoes, a pair of house shoes, a pair of white summer shoes and a pair of spats.

This girl always has at least three pairs of shoes in wear, and never puts on the same two days running—a plan which greatly lengthens the life of footwear and also keeps the feet in good condition. Of course this budget shows individual peculiarities and can only be taken as a general guide. Other girls will probably spend less on their corsets, for instance, and save by wearing lisle stockings all or part of the time, whereas she wears cashmere practically all the year round. On the other hand, her shoe, frock and cleaning bills are unusually small.

It is always wise to have a second odd skirt, apart from the one belonging to your costume. It can be worn under a long coat in winter and with a sports coat in summer, also on many indoor occasions, thus extending the life of the costume, of which the skirt part always wears out first. If a costume is to be worn for a year or more, it should be of a plain, neat cut that does not date quickly.

Commissionaires, tram conductors, lady chauffeurs and others who wear a uniform provided by their employers, will naturally be able to save somewhat on their dress bills, and need a smaller allowance in proportion to their incomes. Women who are on their feet all day, as is the case with farm workers, lady postmen, &c., will have to spend extra on boots, as these get such heavy wear. They should always wear stockings with woollen feet, as the all-cotton ones are most tiring when standing a lot. Cashmere stockings are hot in summer, but a kind with woollen feet and cotton legs is now sold, and costs less than the all-wool variety.

Every woman worker, whatever her trade, should make it a rule to wear pure wool combinations, with fairly high neck and sleeves to the elbow, next to the skin in winter. With this protection it does not matter much how few or how light are the garments worn above. During the summer a silk and wool mixture without sleeves may replace the heavier make, but cotton should never be worn next to the skin. It is liable to cause severe chills.

This article is necessarily of a rather general nature, as clothes vary so much according to the amount of the allowance, the occupations, residence in town or country, and amusements. It is well to remember that elaborate clothes and fine effects are not considered good taste in war-time, whereas one can be seen anywhere in these strenuous days dressed in a neat costume, with a fresh blouse and hat. "When in doubt, underdress," is a safe motto for to-day.

DRESS CARE AND CLEANING

To be always well-dressed on a small allowance, it is necessary not only to choose clothes carefully, but to look after them well. As much economy can be effected by regular brushing, cleaning, pressing and hanging of garments, as by any other means.

Skirts, coats, frocks and easily crushed blouses should always be hung when not in wear, as, if folded and laid away in a drawer, they so quickly get creased and lose their smartness. If you have no wardrobe, curtain off a recess and fix hooks in it. These curtain wardrobes are usually far from dustproof, so the clothes hung in them should be protected by being shrouded in old nightgowns or long calico bags. Unbleached calico at $2\frac{3}{4}$d. a yard is excellent for making protectors.

Coats, frocks and blouses should hang on wooden hangers, which hold out the shoulders in the natural position and preserve the shape of the garments. Hangers cost only about 2d. each, and you should have quite half a dozen.

Walking skirts should be kept for outdoor wear only, as they quickly sag at the knees if used for sitting in. It is an economy and not an extravagance to have a second skirt for indoor wear, so that the one belonging to your costume may last as long as possible.

After being out on a muddy day, you should brush the skirt you have worn as soon as the mud has dried. Coats and woollen frocks should also be thoroughly brushed from time to time, if they are to keep their freshness.

Have a thin, soft hat brush as well as a clothes brush, and brush your hats when you take them off, especially if they are covered ones in dark colours, which show the dust quickly. Black velvet and satin hats need particular care in this respect. Hats must always be kept in big, deep hat boxes when not in wear.

Boots and shoes last best if they are kept on trees or have the toes well stuffed with soft paper. The floor of the wardrobe is a good place for storing footwear. Light-coloured shoes keep clean longer, however, wrapped in tissue paper, and placed in cardboard boxes with well-fitting lids.

Home Cleaning Hints.

Many girls have larger cleaner's bills than they need, because they are under the impression that such-and-such a fabric will not wash, when in reality it takes quite kindly to the tub. Nowadays stuffs have improved so much that there are very few which will not wash, the chief of those few being chiffon, ninon, velvet, velveteen (sometimes), cloth and some satins and silks.

Serge and tweed wash excellently, and do not spoil in the least, but they generally shrink, and coats are apt to get out of shape. Skirts, however, especially if unlined, need only doing carefully at home.

A few velveteens launder, but as a rule this material must be dry-cleaned. A scrap should always be tried in the washtub before risking the garment itself.

Georgette crêpe washes beautifully, and it is a waste of money to have blouses of this lovely fabric cleaned.

Crêpe de chine always washes well, unless it is a very poor quality. It pays to buy an expensive make, as it will wash and wash until entirely worn out. Care must be taken with delicate colours to avoid their running.

Wool-backed or Roman satin will wash very well, but the silk and cotton-backed varieties must go to the cleaner.

Japanese silk is a splendid washing material, and so is *tussore*. Most other silks need cleaning. It is well worth while to have white silk shirts cleaned the first time; then, however often they are washed subsequently, they will not turn yellow.

Of course no delicate or doubtful materials should be sent to a laundry, but washed carefully at home with Lux.

Petrol is useful for cleaning white silk and silk trimming. Dab the silk up and down in petrol until clean, squeezing but never rubbing the material; then hang it out to dry in the open air. Blouses cleaned in this way do not need ironing. Petrol is also useful for taking out stains on serge, but as it is highly inflammable it must never be used near a fire or naked light.

Navy or black serge which has become shiny after much wear may be wonderfully freshened by sponging it over with ammonia and water. The same solution makes black moiré look as good as new.

White kid, canvas or poplin shoes are easily cleaned with whitening and water, rubbed on with a bit of flannel and left to dry, or with one of the ready-prepared cleansers sold everywhere.

A cloth ball, costing 3d. or 6d. from a chemist, lasts a long time and is a splendid cleanser for white felt hats, white and light-coloured cloth or tweed costumes, skirts, coats, &c. White straw hats which are soiled and sunburnt may be whitened by rubbing over with lemon juice.

How to Remove Stains from Clothes.

Inkstains will come out if they are soaked *at once* in a saucer of milk. If the stains are not treated until they have dried, milk is useless, but spirits of salt will remove the mark, though it also tends to rot the stuff. N.B. Spirits of salt is poisonous. A paste made of kitchen salt and lemon juice is recommended by some people, but I have not found it efficacious.

Tea and cocoa stains must be washed out first in cold water as far as possible and then plunged in boiling water, if the stuff is white.

Coffee stains are best removed by pouring boiling water through the stain into a basin underneath. If the stuff will not stand this treatment, the stain is a very difficult one to deal with.

Grass stains can seldom resist being damped with cold water, covered with cream of tartar and set in the sun for half an hour.

A grease stain may be treated by covering the mark with a paste made of fuller's earth and cold water. Allow this to dry on, then brush it off, and renew the process until all the grease has been absorbed. The fuller's earth does not hurt coloured material in the least.

A blood stain needs soaking for a time in cold salt and water, to loosen it, and then washing out in soapy water.

An oil stain made by machine oil yields to being covered with lard, and afterwards washed, first with cold, and then with hot water and soap, but I am inclined to consider salad oil stains quite hopeless.

HOME DYEING.

Now that dyes can be bought for a few pence each, home dyeing is a notable economy for girls to practise. Light-coloured blouses, cotton frocks, &c., take on a new lease of life when their faded looks are hidden in a dye of some deeper shade, or are retinted the same colour. By carefully following the directions which accompany the dyes you are sure of success.

White or light-coloured poplin shoes may be made more useful wear by being painted over with hat dye in a dark shade. Hats which have lost colour can be retinted with the same mixture, and thereby greatly improved.

ETIQUETTE FOR THE WOMAN
WORKER

When dealing with employers or fellow-workers who are men, *try to forget that you are a woman.* Girls who fill men's places and feel aggrieved if they are not paid equal salaries, must not expect privileges on account of their sex which the men do not obtain. Do not claim in business any of the little distinctions which belong to ladies socially. If they are offered, accept gratefully; if not, don't look or feel resentful.

Be respectful to your employer; it is not lowering your dignity in the least to speak to him deferentially, to stand aside to let him pass, open the door for him (or her) and so forth. Never interrupt when your employer is speaking, either to yourself or to someone else. If you have to take a message to him while he is engaged in conversation, stand quietly waiting until he speaks to you, which he will probably do in the first convenient pause.

To be asked out to lunch by your employer, or to his house, is a mark of favour which should not be declined unless absolutely necessary. Such invitations often lead to the offer of a better post or something equally advantageous.

If your employer rings or sends for you, go at once, or promptly at the time appointed. Always knock at his door before entering.

If you and your employer are already friends before you start working for him, try to keep strictly to business matters during working hours.

Working for anyone does not entitle you to the free use of his telephone and stationery, as many girls, especially those in offices, seem to think. Never use your employer's telephone without having first received permission, and don't ask for that permission oftener than you can help. If you have opportunities of writing private letters in working hours (which is not often the case) keep some of your own stationery where it will be available. Do not ask your friends to send letters to you at your business address or to ring you up there; most employers dislike this extremely, even if they are too courteous to say so.

How to Word Business Letters.

A good letter, well expressed, concise and correctly framed, is often such a help in securing a post that you should know the etiquette of business correspondence. It is quite simple.

A business letter begins with "Sir" or "Madam," or more usually, "Dear Sir" or "Dear Madam." If addressing a firm, the correct plural is not "Dear Sirs," as so commonly used, but "Gentlemen." The usual endings for business letters are "Yours faithfully" or "Yours truly." "Yours very truly" may be used when the parties concerned are acquainted with one another.

A letter beginning "Sir" or "Dear Sir" is addressed on the envelope to A. E. Jones, Esq., using the correct initials; or —Jones, Esq., if they are unknown. A firm is addressed as Messrs. Jones & Brown, or Messrs. The Soap Manufacturing Company. Usually only initials, not the Christian name, are signed in business letters. If writing to people who do not know whether you are unmarried or not, put Miss in brackets before your name, thus: (Miss) M. Smith. It is very bad form to omit the brackets.

Be sure to date a business letter correctly, giving the month, day of month and year. Many people have an idea that there is no need to date a postcard, but it is much better to do so.

Letters of application for a post should be as short as is consistent with giving *all* the information asked for. Don't waste words in such vague phrases as, "I am sure I could give you satisfaction," which mean nothing.

Letters to shops are often written in the third person, and are addressed to Mr. Jones, instead of to A. E. Jones, Esq.

Always answer business letters promptly.

Social Etiquette.

Outside working hours ordinary social etiquette prevails, and a girl worker moves on equal terms with those who may be her superiors in a business way. At a social function men under whom she works should pay her all the little courtesies due to a lady.

A girl is not expected to return the hospitalities of much older or married friends, though she may present flowers, or Christmas or birthday gifts occasionally as marks of her appreciation, and perform any little services that come her way. You should always open doors and gates for older ladies, and stand aside to let them pass out before you.

When making introductions, remember that the gentleman is presented to the lady, no matter if she is the younger, and the girl to the married or older woman. The name of the superior of the two people always comes last; thus, "Mr. Jones—Miss Smith"; "Miss Smith—Mrs. Brown."

If you are introduced to someone of whom you have heard a great deal, or with whom you are likely to become intimate, it is usual to shake hands; otherwise simply bow and smile. You should rise when being introduced to an older lady, but need not do so if a gentleman is presented.

Bachelor girls are too apt to fall into free and easy ways and to think introductions may be dispensed with, but this is a very serious mistake that may lead to terrible trouble. A girl who lives alone and has no one to look after her cannot be too careful regarding the men (and women) with whom she associates. People who are willing to waive introductions are rarely desirable companions and should be sternly discouraged.

It is always possible to say pleasantly, "I am sorry but I do not know you. If you could find someone to introduce us——" This generally has the effect of driving away undesirable acquaintances, while those who have erred through carelessness will find means to get a proper introduction.

Girls who go about much alone in big towns (especially in certain parts of London) sometimes complain of being spoken to by strange men. This will rarely, if ever, happen, if you walk along briskly and purposefully, not staring at anyone. It is loitering and aimless strolling that are to be avoided. If spoken to in spite of precautions, a decided answer or a cold stare will usually end the annoyance.

In war-time you are hardly likely to be invited to dances or dinner-parties, but invitations may be received for informal gatherings. The answering of invitations is a snare to many.

An invitation expressed in the third person should be answered in the same way. "Miss Smith thanks Mrs. Robinson for her kind invitation for January 1st, which she has much pleasure in accepting." *Not* "Will have much pleasure in accepting." The accepting is not a future, but a present action. If the invitation begins like a letter with "Dear Miss Brown," it should be answered in the same style.

It is very bad manners to delay in answering an invitation. The reply should be sent the same day or the day after receiving it. If declining an invitation, always state the reason, or you will give the impression that you have refused because you do not care to go.

If you are invited to a wedding, you will be expected to send a present, whether you go or not. Send with the gift a card expressing good wishes, which can be attached to it when it is shown at the reception. Unless you have never met the bride, your present should be sent to her, and not to the bridegroom, even if you know him the better of the two.

Bachelor girls are often invited away for week-ends. If you go to stay with friends take care to be a pleasant guest who will be invited again. There are many little ways in which you can please your hostess.

If she suggests a train, try to go by that one, as no doubt it suits her convenience. Make a point of being punctual at meals, and do not give more trouble than you can help to the servants. If no maids are kept, make your own bed and lend a hand where you can. When your hostess is busy with household affairs, amuse yourself without bothering her to entertain you.

On arriving home after the visit write at once to your hostess, thanking her for the pleasant time you have had.

If your hostess keeps a maid, she must be tipped before you leave, either by putting the money into her hand or by leaving it on the dressing table in your room. Girls are not expected to give such large tips as married women; 1/- or 1/6 is sufficient for a week-end, while 2/6 would be given at the end of a week's visit.

If staying at a hotel you must tip the chamber-maid and the waiter who attends to you when you leave.

Mourning.

Since war started quite a strong feeling has arisen against wearing black for relatives who have died on active service; a black band on the left arm is often the only intimation given. The question of mourning, however, is one of personal preference.

The length of mourning tends to get shorter as time goes on. For a father or mother it lasts a year; during ten months all black is worn, during the last two half-mourning (black and white, grey or mauve). Five months of black and one month of half-mourning are correct for a brother or sister; for brothers or sisters-in-law the mourning is four months (three months of black and one of half-mourning). For a fiancé or grandparent, three months' black and an equal period of half-mourning. For uncles, aunts, nephews, nieces and cousins, two months' black and one month's half-mourning. Only very quiet jewellery (preferably jet) should be worn during mourning.

Visitors and Hospitality.

Every girl likes to entertain her friends from time to time, but this is not always an easy matter when she is away from home, and often some contrivance is necessary.

If you live in unfurnished rooms, a flat or a cottage, you are your own mistress as regards visitors and can invite them when you will; the difficulty in this case is more frequently one of accommodation, as a spare room is not often available. The easiest plan is to own a folding bed, which can be put up in your own room when a visitor comes.

Provided you have ample space for furniture, quite the nicest kind of bed to have is the sort which forms a broad settee in the daytime and a bed by night. With the mattress upholstered in some pretty chintz, this can be bought for about £2, and makes a charming piece of sitting-room furniture. When a visitor comes you can give up your bed to her, sleeping yourself on the couch-bed in the sitting-room. Of course, if you have this second bed, it will mean keeping enough bedding for it as well as your own.

Chair bedsteads are a good deal cheaper, but are not so useful or pretty in the daytime. One can be bought second-hand for 7/6 to 12/-.

If you have only one or two rooms and are cramped for space, you will need a visitors' bed which will fold into a corner or under the bed when not in use. A kind which answers these requirements is the Cabinetta bed, a folding wooden affair with a canvas frame to hold the mattress. The latter, stuffed with horsehair, is sold separately, at 6/9, the bed costing from 18/- upwards, according to quality. About a guinea is a satisfactory price to pay. The bed is very narrow and suitable for only occasional use, but it folds up small, and can be used as a seat or stowed away out of sight. Cabinetta beds are stocked by most of the big furniture shops.

If you live in furnished rooms, you will depend for your chance of having friends to stay on your landlady having another bedroom vacant, or on being able to get one in a neighbouring house. The terms paid for a visitor are a matter of arrangement in each case.

Hostels usually make provision for visitors on certain terms, which vary according to the rules of the establishment. Usually there are no rooms reserved for visitors, and they can come only when a bedroom happens to be vacant. In a hostel you would be required to provide towels, serviette and perhaps soap for your guest, but in apartments the landlady sees to these items.

When entertaining a guest in your own flat or independent set of rooms, provide her with two towels—a face towel, and a rougher Turkish one—and a new tablet of soap. Any guest who comes even to a single meal must have a clean serviette, except in the case of tea, when you may either provide a paper one or a little tea serviette.

Have hot water ready for a guest when she arrives, and unless she has free access to the bath-room provide her with more hot water every morning and once or twice during the day.

Holidays.

During absence on holiday rent for your quarters is payable just as usual, but generally speaking some allowance is made for the food which does not have to be provided during your absence. In furnished rooms a definite arrangement should be made with the landlady from the beginning as to holidays, by which in this particular instance I mean all absences, whether for weeks, days or single meals.

If the landlady charges extra when you have a guest to lunch or tea, she should deduct something every time you yourself miss a meal; if she "throws in" meals for guests, you cannot expect a reduction when you are out for the day or evening. During absence from rooms the amount generally expended by her on your food and an allowance for attendance, lights and fuel, should be subtracted from your weekly bill. The same sort of arrangement applies in the case of a paying guest, who should come to a definite agreement on the subject when she enters her new quarters.

In unfurnished rooms or a flat the problem solves itself. You pay your rent as usual, but save the outlay on food, fuel and lighting.

Hostels generally make rather hard terms with their inmates with regard to absences, deducting nothing, or very little, from the full resident payment. In some of these establishments a small weekly sum may be saved during holidays if the tenant is willing for her room to be sub-let to stray visitors; but many girls naturally do not care for this.

POINTS ABOUT CHARWOMEN.

Girls who employ a charwoman to do their household work are usually very ignorant about her rights, wages, &c., so a few words on the subject will probably not be amiss.

The usual plan is for the woman to come in about seven every morning, cook and lay breakfast, and afterwards wash it up, make the beds, and do any necessary sweeping, dusting, &c., before going away. Coming again at five or six in the evening, she prepares, cooks and serves the evening meal and departs after washing up the dishes used for it and any others which may have been soiled during the day. Most charwomen refuse to come in on Sundays, or if they consent, will come only for a little while in the morning to get breakfast and make beds.

For this work the usual weekly wage is from 10/- to 14/-, or less if the woman comes in only once a day.

If a charwoman arrives early in the morning, before the occupants of the flat are up, or comes in the evening while they are still away at work, she will have to be given a latch-key. For this reason great care must be exercised to get an honest, trustworthy person, and she should not be engaged until references have been taken up.

A charwoman is entitled to her full pay during any time when her employer may be away from home. The fact that she has no work to do in their absence does not affect the question.

Many people have the impression that char-women (and maids) are liable to pay for breakages for which they are responsible. This is an entire mistake. You cannot legally deduct anything from a charwoman's wages for articles she has broken; your only remedy is to get rid of her.

If a charwoman is paid by the week she is entitled to a week's notice or a week's pay. Should she wish to leave you, you are entitled to a week's notice; should she leave without giving this notice, you need not pay any wages that may be owing.

You are required to pay the employer's share of your charwoman's national insurance, and to see that her card is properly stamped, with the date written across each stamp. Full particulars with regard to this will be found on her card.

HOW TO TREAT SMALL AILMENTS

A slight knowledge of home doctoring is useful to all of us, especially nowadays, when doctors are worked so hard that we hesitate to call them in for small matters. If, however, your temperature is decidedly above the average, it is always wisest to seek medical advice.

A clinical thermometer is a most useful possession if you are not very strong, as with it you can take your own temperature, and judge whether the indisposition is more than slight. Put the thermometer into your mouth, under the tongue, and leave it there for four or five minutes, taking care not to bite it with your teeth. Then take it out and see how high the mercury comes on the scale.

The normal temperature of the human body is 98.8 degrees, but very slight causes may raise it to 99 degrees even in a person of sound health, and temperature always rises a little towards the evening. If the temperature is over 99 the patient should stop in bed until it returns to normal.

After each use the thermometer requires shaking down to normal, and this is done with a wrist movement that is rather difficult to acquire. Cold water has not the slightest effect in bringing down the level of the mercury.

Aches of many kinds, such as ear-ache, face-ache and so on, are best cured by the application of heat to the affected part. An indiarubber hot water bottle wrapped in flannel may be used, or a hot fomentation, which consists of a piece of linen wrung out of almost boiling water, laid on the ache, and secured round with a warm woollen bandage. A magic cure for earache is a flannel bag filled with hot salt (heated in the oven) and laid on the pillow, with the affected ear over it.

Biliousness shows that the liver is out of order, and for this reason diet is most important. As long as any feeling of sickness lasts you should take no food whatever, but lie down, warmly covered, and try to sleep. Sympathising friends often urgently offer cups of tea, but these are likely to aggravate matters. Do not take anything until you feel really hungry again, and then let it be warm milk diluted with soda-water. Cold milk is less easily digested. Girls with bilious tendencies should eat plain food, and avoid as far as possible eggs, pastry, cream, cucumber, pickles, &c.

Constipation is a complaint which must be attended to, as if neglected it becomes chronic and brings many other evils in its train. Do not get into the habit of taking aperients regularly, or after a time they will cease to have an effect, and so will have to be made stronger and stronger.

Much can be done by careful dieting. If you suffer from this complaint drink between, rather than at, meals, and take a glass of hot water immediately after rising every morning. Remember that milk (especially when cold), tea, white bread and starchy foods generally, make matters worse, but that green vegetables, fruit (all kinds but bananas, but especially oranges, prunes and figs), hot drinks and brown bread are beneficial. Breakfast should begin with fruit, as it loses much of its effect if taken after other food. Exercises which act upon the muscles in the lower part of the body often do a great deal of good.

Diarrhœa is most common in hot weather, and is often brought on by excessive indulgence in raw fruit, or by a chill. Avoid all fruit, green vegetables and jam until the attack is over, and live mainly upon milk and white bread and butter. Take as little exercise as possible, and if the bout is severe stay in bed and keep very warm.

Headaches are due to so many different causes that it is absurd to treat them all in the same way, by taking Aspirin or some other remedy of the same kind, which, though giving momentary relief, does not remove the *cause* of a headache, and leaves a feeling of depression behind. Headaches may be caused by insufficient ventilation, by piercing winds blowing in one's face, by indigestion, biliousness, constipation, excitement and so on. In most of these instances the remedy is obvious. A veil gives a good deal of protection from cold winds, and the outsides of buses should be avoided.

A headache brought on by excitement can usually be cured by lying down in a darkened room. Another source of headache is eyestrain, and if you often have pain immediately over the eyes when working or reading, you will do well to have your eyes tested.

Sore Throat, like headache, is due to many different causes. There are two distinct kinds of sore throat; *sore*, when it feels rough, scratchy, and inflamed, and it is painful to eat, though liquids can be swallowed easily; and *relaxed*, characterised by a steady aching feeling, but no roughness, and when taking liquids is more painful than taking solids. If the throat is relaxed, yawning and gulping movements are generally very painful.

A sore throat may be due to a chill, a bad cough which inflames the throat, poison of some kind (such as a bad smell or an open drain), or it may be an early symptom in influenza, scarlet fever, German measles or diphtheria. If you have been exposed to the risk of any of these complaints, you should be very suspicious of a sore throat. Gargling is the best throat remedy, and you should gargle three or four times a day with hot water in which you have dissolved either a couple of grains of permanganate of potash, or half a teaspoonful of borax.

A relaxed throat generally shows that you are below par in some way; it often occurs in very hot weather, or if you have been worried or overworked. If it does not go away after a day or two of its own accord, take a bottle of tonic or try to get a little holiday. Go to bed early, and lead a quiet life for a while.

Sore or Watering Eyes should never be neglected, for good sight is so infinitely precious to a working girl. If the eyes water without reason or are sore, bloodshot or have crusted lashes when you wake in the morning, they are in a weak condition and need strengthening. You can do this by bathing them every night and morning for several weeks in cold tea, which is an excellent astringent. Use a bit of soft old rag for dabbing on the tea, and burn each bit after use. The same rag must not be used for both eyes, or infection may be carried from one to the other.

Sprains and Strains such as are caused by a sudden awkward movement, are often decidedly painful. Rubbing is the best treatment for them. Moisten the hand with some embrocation, and rub it over the sore part until all the liquid is well rubbed in. Do this twice a day until the pain disappears.

CARPENTERING JOBS IN THE HOUSE

Since in your bachelor establishment there is no man to wield a hammer and screwdriver on your behalf, you should have a working acquaintance with these and other tools, for little jobs are always cropping up that are hardly worthy of the attention of professional carpenters.

If a room has no picture rail and pictures have consequently to be suspended from nails, there is often trouble in indifferently built houses from the plaster crumbling away and making a hole when the nail is hammered in. To remedy this defect, buy a little plaster of Paris, drive in the nail, and fill the gap round it with plaster. The latter will set as hard as a rock, and hold the nail with absolute security. If the mark shows very much, and you have a spare piece of wallpaper, tear a little bit the right size to cover it and paste it over the place. I say *tear*, not cut, for torn edges are much less noticeable than cut ones.

In a room where there is a precious piece of furniture behind the door, it is a good plan to fix a door-stop, which will prevent the door, when carelessly flung open, from hitting and disfiguring the furniture, or marking a new wallpaper. The stop must be fixed to the floor a few inches in front of the object to be protected. It is simply an odd little bit of wood, about 1½ inches square and ½ inch thick, fastened to the floor with a French nail. To make it less noticeable, a scrap of felt or cloth, the same colour as the carpet may be glued to its surface; or, in the case of a polished floor, the stop should be stained to match the boards as nearly as possible.

Often in old-fashioned houses with large windows the sashes are so heavy that it is a great strain on feminine muscles to throw them up and down when opening and closing the windows. As all forms of stretching and straining are apt to be most injurious to a girl, it is well worth while to remedy the bother by adding cords and a pulley to each troublesome window.

For a penny or two you can buy a suitable pulley at the ironmonger's, and you will also need two yards of stout window-cord. Fix the pulley with a couple of wire nails to the top of the sash, about in the centre, and put the cord over it so that it will run easily along the groove in the pulley. Knot the two ends of the cord firmly through a little ring fixed in the top of the window sash, and by pulling one cord or the other, the window will fly up and down without any difficulty.

It pays to make window boxes at home, as they are rather expensive to buy. The best wood to use is $\frac{1}{2}$ inch thick deal, 9 inches wide, which costs a few pence a foot from your local carpenter. For an average-sized window the box will take about $7\frac{1}{2}$ feet of wood, likely dimensions being 2 feet long, 9 inches wide and 6 inches deep.

With a ruler and sharply pointed pencil, begin by measuring the wood into the various lengths required—two sides, each 2 feet by 6 inches; two ends, each 9 inches by 6 inches, and one bottom, measuring 1 foot 11 inches by 8 inches.

Of course you have not got a proper carpenter's bench on which to saw up your pieces, but you can use a pair of trestles or two kitchen chairs as substitutes. Lay the board across them, and steady it either with your left knee or your left hand, while you hold the saw in the right hand. The board must project one side some inches further than the line along which you are sawing.

To put the pieces together after all are measured and cut, lay the bottom flat on your work table and put the two sides in position *against* it—not *on* it—so that the bottom edges of the sides rest on the table, not on the bottom of the window box. This is the reason why the bottom is cut an inch short each way—to allow for the thickness of the wood twice over.

Nail the sides carefully into position, using headless French nails, and driving them in until their tops are flush with the wood and do not project in the least. Three nails, one at each end and one in the middle, will be needed to secure each side to the bottom. Then the two ends can be similarly nailed in place, and the box painted inside and out with a dark green stain.

For window box plants and their cultivation, see the next page.

WINDOW BOX GARDENING

Very few bachelor girls have even the smallest plot of ground for gardening, and yet the love of flowers and growing things is inherent in practically every woman. This is where window boxes prove their value, for they form tiny gardens and spots of bright colour for flat-dwellers and those in rooms.

It is a good plan, before filling the boxes with earth, to bore several holes in them with the carpentering tool known as a brace-and-bit, or failing that, with a poker heated red-hot in the fire. Then cover the bottom of the box with crocks (broken bits of a flower-pot) and good drainage is assured.

If you have not access to a garden from which you can get soil for your boxes, you will have to buy some from a nurseryman. The soil chosen should be fairly light.

The plants that will thrive in your boxes depend upon the aspect of the window. North or east exposures are far less favourable than south and west ones, owing to the cold winds which blow from the first-named quarters.

CHOICE OF PLANTS.

For cold aspects fuchsias, calceolarias, begonias

and white and yellow marguerites are the most suitable, and all do well in north and east windows. Another good plant is the pretty campanula isophylla, which has charming white blossoms. When choosing begonias for window boxes select single varieties with medium-sized blossoms, as they do better and flower more profusely than the larger kinds.

For warm aspects you will be safe in choosing double geraniums, which are perhaps the best of all plants for window boxes, and can be got in all shades from a deep, rich red to the palest salmon pink. Lobelias are also good, but they should not be mixed with geraniums, as the colour effect is then anything but pretty.

These suggestions are, of course, for the summer months, but if window boxes are to look nice all the year round, you will have to plant several crops at different seasons. In the autumn the boxes are charming filled with hardy chrysanthemums. The dwarf varieties are the best and make a very good show until well into November. On frosty nights they should be covered with several layers of newspaper, which affords a surprising amount of heat.

As soon as the chrysanthemums are over, bulbs should be put in for late winter flowering. Crocuses, starch hyacinths, daffodils, hyacinths and tulips are all suitable, and should be carefully planted so that the colour effects will be good, as most bulbs are somewhat gaudy. These give place in the second half of May (or the beginning of June in northern counties) to the summer plants already suggested.

As the bulbs planted in the autumn do not begin to make a show till February or March, it is advisable to have one or two other things in each box to give a pleasant green look during December and January. Polypody ferns are evergreen, and thrive facing all points of the compass, while yellow jasmine flowers in mid-winter, when no other blossoms are out. In a warm box with a western exposure retinosporas make a pretty show during the cold months of the year. Dwarf wallflowers, which bloom in early spring, may be mingled with the bulbs, while perennial candytuft, flowering rather later, will fill the gap between the spring bulbs and summer blossoms.

Window boxes are always prettiest from the outside if trailing plants grow round the edges. Tradescantia is a pretty trailer which grows rapidly, and combines particularly well with geraniums. The variegated tradescantia is another good choice, but is less hardy and requires plenty of sun.

Window boxes must be kept very neat, or they will be ugly instead of beautiful. See that they are always well watered, and use only artificial manure, such as guano, and not too much of that. If you want your window boxes to be useful and economical, instead of merely ornamental, you can grow crops of mustard and cress, radishes and lettuce in them, from April to September.

Indoor Plants.

There are very few women who do not have

something growing in their rooms, and besides the interest of watching the plants, their greenery is always decorative and saves money spent on cut flowers.

Perhaps the favourite plants of all are aspidistras, and these are certainly very hardy, though not particularly beautiful. Palms also flourish well indoors, and so do aralias, except in rooms heated or lighted by gas. Other good room plants are the hare's food fern, the davallia, the asparagus fern and the eucalyptus plant. Spring is the best time of year for buying indoor plants.

The Proper Way to Water.

Naturally watering is very important in the case of room plants, which cannot get their moisture from the rain, like those out of doors. The golden rule in watering is to wait until the plant really needs it and then to do it thoroughly. Frequent sprinkles which only wet the top layer of soil are of little or no use. If, when you tap the pot sharply, it gives out a ringing sound, then water is needed; if the sound is dull, the plant is moist enough. When a plant has been properly watered the water will run out into the saucer underneath the pot, showing that every particle of soil has been penetrated and moistened.

Plants which live in a warm room thrive much better if the water given to them is warm, or at any rate, has the chill taken off. If the room is a cold one, cold water is preferable. Large-leaved plants, such as aspidistras, should have only the roots watered, as if the foliage is wetted the drops of moisture turn the leaves yellow, and rot them. Large-leaved plants also require a weekly sponging to keep the foliage free of dust, and this should always be done with gloved hands, for the reason that contact with the human skin turns the leaves yellow and quite spoils their appearance. Aspidistra leaves also shrivel and discolour if they are allowed to come into contact with surrounding objects, such as furniture or curtains.

Saucers standing under pots should be emptied about an hour after watering, except in very hot weather or in the case of certain ferns, which flourish better if the pots are always standing in water. In winter under-water rather than over-water indoor plants.

As plants always grow towards the light, it is important to turn them round frequently, or they will grow all to one side and soon get deformed.

Re-Potting.

Most owners of indoor plants re-pot rather too zealously. Unless this operation is very carefully done, it is a loss rather than a gain to the plant. Palms hardly ever require re-potting, as they do best in small pots, but some plants (the aspidistra is one) need re-potting every year. It is most important to re-pot only during the months of February, March, April and May.

See that the new pot is perfectly clean and dry. Peat, loam and sand in equal parts form the best potting soil, with the addition of a little leaf mould (which you can buy, or collect from a wood) in the case of ferns. If you like you can buy a ready-mixed potting soil, costing about 1/- a peck, from any seedsman. Put clean crocks at the bottom of the pot to keep the soil sweet, and shake the pot occasionally while filling, so that every crevice may be filled. When the pot is filled to within an inch of the top (in a large pot) or half an inch (in a small one) *press the mould down very firmly.*

A layer of coconut fibre put over the top of the soil neatens the appearance of the pot and sets off the foliage to advantage. Threepence will purchase enough fibre to last for many months.

EVERYDAY MONEY MATTERS

For some obscure reason simple facts about money matters never seem to be taught at schools, and the consequence is that a girl often sets out to make her own way in the world without the most elementary knowledge about such everyday matters as the drawing of a cheque, or the making out of a receipt, and thus falls a ready prey to dishonest people.

Make a point of getting a receipt for all payments you make. If you have weekly rent to pay, you can buy for a penny a card marked out for the whole year, with a space each week for the amount paid and the initials of the receiver. Failing such a convenient card, get a receipt, stating the amount of money paid, the date, and giving the signature of your creditor (or whoever took the money) each week. If you make out the receipt yourself, the person taking it will need only to sign it, and will have no excuse for postponing this simple operation.

Of course I do not mean to imply that you are likely to be cheated. The vast majority of people are perfectly honest, but business is business, and it is much wiser to be on the safe side.

If when shopping you pay for goods that are to be delivered later, make sure that the bill you take with you is receipted, as it is your only proof that you have paid for the goods. Tradesmen's books, all paid bills and so on, must be duly receipted at the time of paying.

In the same way you must give receipts yourself for payments made to you. If you are a regular employee, you probably have to sign for your salary each time you receive it, but if you are doing independent work, such as typing manuscripts, dressmaking or translating, you will have to make out accounts for the people for whom you work. When these are paid, do not omit to write "Received with thanks," the date and your signature across the bill, and to return it to the payer. If you are sending a receipt through the post, remember that it will go for a halfpenny if you turn the flap of the envelope in, instead of sealing it.

It is important to note that *receipts for amounts of £2 or over are not valid unless stamped with a penny stamp*, which is provided and affixed by the person who receives the money.

If you have received money by post, always acknowledge it at once, either by writing or by sending a formal receipt. If you do not have an acknowledgement of money sent by you within a reasonable time, be sure to inquire whether it has reached its destination. The Post Office is not liable for money lost in transit unless the letter containing it was registered.

A tradesman or other person is not bound to accept a cheque in payment of an account. He may do so if he pleases, but he has the right to demand payment in cash, for a cheque is not cash, but only an order on a bank to pay the money.

Opening a Banking Account.

Not many girls have any occasion to do this, if they are paid their salaries in cash, and have no considerable savings or private means. But when a girl gets on in the world, and begins to put by a good part of her earnings, a banking account is convenient and useful; and it becomes practically essential if money payments are made to her by means of crossed cheques or postal orders, as happens often in the case of women journalists, artists, &c.

A crossed postal order or cheque (i.e. one which has two parallel lines drawn across it, either diagonally or vertically) can be paid through a banking account only, hence if you get money habitually in this form you must either have a banking account of your own, or get a friend to pay it through his or hers. The latter method is all right for occasional cheques, but it gets very tiresome and complicated if there are many.

To open a banking account, choose one of the well-known banks which has a branch conveniently placed for your home or business address, and apply to the manager. You will have to give references—if possible, get someone who is already a client at the same branch to introduce you to the manager. You should have a sum of not less than £10—preferably more—available to open your account, and you will be asked to sign your ordinary signature once or twice in the bank's books, so that they may have something with which to compare the signatures on your cheques, to guard against forgery. You will also receive a cheque book, for which your account will be debited a penny per cheque. You will be asked whether you prefer "order" or "bearer" cheques. Be sure to choose the former, as they are so much safer.

The bank will provide you with a paying-in book, filled with a number of perforated slips. You enter particulars as to the date, your name and the amounts paid in on both the counter-foil and the slip, and take the book with you when you go to pay in cheques. The cashier will mark the counterfoil to show that he has received the money, tear out the slip and return you the book.

How to Draw a Cheque.

If you wish to take money out of the bank you must draw a cheque. Write the date in the space provided at the top, and fill in the name of the payee, with the amount below, first in words and then in figures. Then sign your usual signature in the lower right-hand corner. By your usual signature I mean the one you signed in the bank's books when opening your account. If you signed "Mary A. Jones" then, you must always stick to it, not vary by sometimes putting "M. A. Jones" or "Mary Ann Jones"

If you are drawing a cheque which you intend to cash yourself, write "Self" in the space reserved for the name of the payee, and sign the cheque also on the back. This is called endorsing, and all cheques you receive must be endorsed before you pay them in. In this case sign just as the cheque is made out. For instance, if it is made payable to "M. A. Jones," endorse it "M. A. Jones," although this is not your usual signature. If you like you can sign your ordinary signature underneath as well.

Always cross cheques which are to be sent by post.

The bank will provide you with a pass-book, in which they enter all amounts paid in and drawn out, and make up the balance at the end of each quarter. You can have your pass-book any time simply by asking for it, if you wish to see how your account stands. It is as well to get it every month or two, in order to check possible inaccuracies by comparing the entries with the counterfoils of your paying-in and cheque books. Most banks slip your old cheques into the inside pocket of the pass-book, and these you should remove and keep.

Always return your pass-book to the bank at the end of March, June, September and December, so that it may be balanced.

Unless you are able to keep what the bank considers a remunerative balance always on the deposit (and this is hardly likely in the early days of your banking account) you will be charged for the bank's trouble in keeping the account. Very likely this charge will be a guinea a year, but it varies according to the size of the balance and the amount of work you cause.

Keep your cheque book locked up, as, if any unscrupulous person obtained possession of it, he would have the means to commit forgery.

LAUNDRY MATTERS

You can send your weekly wash either to a private laundress who takes in washing for a few families, or to a regular steam laundry. As a rule the former is somewhat cheaper, while the latter does better work and is more reliable.

Laundry prices have risen fully 10 per cent during the war, and you will find this an item on which strict economy must be practised. You can wash at home for yourself little articles such as stockings, handkerchiefs and collars.

Nightgowns cost a penny less to have laundered than pyjamas, and cami-knickers work out less than these two garments separately. Thrift can often be effected in the washing of tablecloths if small traycloths, which can be washed at home, are placed over them to take most of the stains. White bedspreads are expensive to keep clean, and should be replaced by covers of coloured casement cloth (see page 31).

All articles returned from the laundry should, as a precautionary measure, be aired before they are used.

How to Wash Stockings.

Soak the stockings for half an hour in a basin

full of warm, soapy water, worked to a good lather. Some people add borax or ammonia to the water, but this is not really necessary.

When the stockings have soaked dab them about in the water and rub them until quite clean, but do not rub the soap directly on to the wool. The soap in the water is sufficient to cleanse them properly.

Rinse well in a basin of clean warm water, wring out as much water as possible, and dry preferably in the open air. Stockings dried at a fire are far more likely to shrink than those hung out of doors.

How to Wash Handkerchiefs.

Put them into a basin of hot water, and soap well, rubbing them until they are quite clean. If you do washing regularly at home, you should keep a special big stewpan or fish kettle for boiling white goods. Fill this with water, let it come to the boil, put in the handkerchiefs (after rinsing) and leave them to boil briskly for half an hour.

Handkerchiefs are not starched. When they are nearly dry iron them, always ironing the border all round first.

How to Wash Muslin Collars.

The fine muslin and organdy collars which are worn so much are rather fragile, and for this reason it is much better to wash them at home. Such small items are very little trouble to get up successfully.

Wash, rinse and boil the collars in the same way as handkerchiefs. These collars are best if starched a little, but they must not be made really stiff, or they will be both ugly and uncomfortable. A recipe for thin starch is given below. Iron the collars carefully, pulling out any lace edges, and taking care to crease them exactly where the stuff turns over, and in no other place.

Recipe for Thin Starch.

Mix one tablespoonful of starch to a fairly thin paste with *absolutely boiling* water. About one pint will be needed. Mix very gently, or the starch will become lumpy. Dip the collar or other article into the starch so that every portion of the stuff is saturated, then take it out, wring it carefully and put it to dry.

This starch is suitable for lawn and muslin blouses as well as collars; in fact, for every article requiring to be only lightly starched.

Blouses.

Cotton blouses must be washed quickly with dissolved soap and warm water, and rinsed in cold water. If the blouse is coloured and there is any risk of fading, add to the rinsing water for a pink or red blouse, a tablespoonful of pure vinegar; for a mauve blouse, a tablespoonful of dissolved lump ammonia; for a blue blouse, two lumps of alum.

Colours may also be safeguarded by being soaked for an hour before they are washed in a solution of salt and water.

Voile blouses are best ironed when quite wet. The hot iron almost dries the thin material, and they will only require a good airing afterwards.

Lawn blouses may be treated in the same way, though some people prefer them thinly starched.

Tussore silk blouses look best if not actually starched, but rolled up for an hour or two with other starched articles. This gives them just the slightest stiffness, which causes them to hang nicely and shows up the full beauty of the stuff.

Cotton blouses are generally ironed on the right side, *flannel and silk* ones on the wrong, but some people iron all blouses on the wrong side. A sleeve board, costing about 2/-, is the greatest aid in ironing a blouse, as it does away with the ugly crease down the outside of the sleeve.

TYPEWRITING

Shorthand-typists, clerks, secretaries, book-keepers, journalists, insurance employees, girls who take in typewriting to do at home and many other kinds of women workers, all need, or are the more useful and consequently more valuable for, a sound knowledge of typewriting. In fact, it is such a generally useful accomplishment to the woman wage-earner in the business world that it is worth her while to go a little out of her way to acquire this particular asset.

This is not an expensive or tedious matter. Typewriting is one of the very few things that can be quite as efficiently learnt by self-tuition as under a teacher. Given the opportunity to use a machine regularly, and an ordinary amount of intelligence (backed by an adequate knowledge of English grammar, spelling and composition) any girl can make herself a satisfactory typist, with the aid of the following instructions.

The best method of teaching yourself type-writing, supposing that you have made up your mind to learn at home, is to buy a second-hand machine, so that you can practise at any time. The amount saved from taking lessons will pay a large part of its cost. For a reliable typewriter you should pay from four to ten pounds, according to make and condition. If you choose a well-known make, such as the Remington or Underwood, it is not necessary that the machine should be one of the latest models. Those of a few years back are cheaper, and in some ways preferable for beginners, as the up-to-date improvements on the newest typewriters complicate the mechanism and make them more difficult for a novice to operate.

Failing the necessary lump sum to buy a machine outright, you can either hire one, pay a small sum for the use of one for a fixed period daily while the owner is not using it, or rely upon the good offices of a typist friend.

If you buy a machine, you must provide a suitable table and chair. The machine should have a table to itself—a small bamboo one, costing three or four shillings, is excellent. The chair should be higher than for writing at a table; bentwood chairs are usually just right, or an ordinary cane-seated one may be raised with a substantial cushion. To sit too low at a typewriter means that you have not full control over the keys, and consequently will tire yourself very quickly.

Now let us suppose that you are duly provided with a machine and wish to set to work. The chief secret of learning well and quickly is to practise for a *regular period daily*. Once or twice a week is very little good, and hours of work at these comparatively rare intervals will not

accomplish as much as twenty or thirty minutes
every day.

How to Begin.

Sit down at your typewriter, not too close to it,
and spend a few minutes studying the keyboard,
as the rows of letters just under your hand are
called. You will notice at once that the letters are
not arranged in alphabetical order.

The diagram (p. 149) shows the Standard Keyboard, which is the arrangement you will find on
nine out of ten machines. The Standard is what is
known as a single keyboard—that is, there are
only four rows of keys, and each key is good for
two different letters, signs or figures.

Many machines have double keyboards; that
is, each key works only one letter, figure or sign,
and consequently many more keys are needed.
Usually in the case of a double keyboard, however, the alphabet is arranged as in the diagram,
and only the figures and punctuation vary from
the recognised arrangement.

Some typists prefer the double, some the single,
keyboard. It is not a matter of great importance,
as very good results can be obtained with either,
provided the make of machine is reliable.

If you play the piano, you will find typewriting
come more easily to you, as the two operations,
viewed from the mechanical aspect, are not unlike.
As when learning music you learnt special fingering for each note, so, in typing, each key has its
own finger, indicated by the numbers 1, 2 and 3
above the keys on the diagram.

You will perceive by this that a typist operates with the first three fingers of each hand. Some teachers recommend using the two little fingers also, but most people agree that this plan is unsatisfactory, owing to the greater shortness and weakness of the fingers in questions. *Many self-taught typists operate only with the two index fingers, but this is the greatest mistake.*

The mechanism of a typewriter varies enormously on the different makes, and you should experiment with the various levers and depressors until you know the use of each.

The diagram indicates the way in which the two hands share the work, the right hand taking the larger half, as it is the stronger. The letter B, you will notice, being just in the centre, may be depressed by which ever hand is most convenient. Coming to individual letters, in the same way, the strong index fingers bear the brunt of the work, with two or three keys in each row, while the weaker second and third fingers are allotted only one apiece.

THE FIRST EXERCISE.

The first thing to learn is to work the keys evenly and to know the place of each on the board. To gain these points devote your first few days of practice to the following exercise:

Depress Q with the third finger of the left hand and continue all along the line to P, using the proper hand and finger in each case. To aid in memorising the keyboard, pronounce each letter aloud as you strike it. Do the same from A to L in the second row and from Z to M in the next. You will notice that in this first exercise the more confusing figures and signs are left severely alone.

When you have done this a number of times, and the sequence of letters sings itself in your head, go over the whole thing again, this time spacing each time you change from the left to the right hand and at the end of each row. A space is made by depressing the space board in front of the keys once. You may use either thumb for the space board, as is most convenient, and thumbs must never be used for anything else.

Next repeat again, making all the letters capitals. How this is done depends on whether your machine has a double or single keyboard.

If a single keyboard: Capitals are printed on the top half of the small letter bars, and are brought into operation by the shift key. The position of the shift key often varies from the places allotted to it on the diagram. Holding down the shift key with the forefinger of one hand, strike the letter with the correct finger; then release the shift key. When a whole row of capitals is to be done, as in the present instance, it is not necessary to hold the shift key down all the time. Either one of the shift keys will stay down when pressed as long as required, or you will find a lever just above the keyboard on the left, which will push up to serve the same purpose.

If a double keyboard: This type of machine has the capitals on separate keys, of a different colour from those which operate the small letters, they are depressed in exactly the same way as the small letter keys.

After becoming thoroughly familiar with the capitals, learn to mix them with the small letters by taking the exercise again, this time beginning after every space with a capital and making the rest of the letters small ones. Finish with a full stop, and gradually accustom yourself to the marks of punctuation. The comma, full stop, dash and semi-colon, on a single-keyboard machine, are lower-case keys; the inverted commas, fraction mark, underline, apostrophe, brackets, question mark, exclamation mark and colon, are on the upper case and worked with the shift key. After a comma, space once before typing the next word; after a colon, semi-colon, exclamation or question mark, space twice; after a full stop, three times.

Exercise II.

This consists of single words, carefully fingered. R and L stand respectively for right and left hands. You will notice that the fingering varies somewhat from that given on the diagram, owing to the fact that it is awkward to use the same finger twice in succession, and therefore fingering must be modified to avoid this. Practise each word along a whole line (spacing between every time) before going on to the next.

LRLLL	LLLL	LRL	RRR	LLL	RRLR	RL
1 1 1 2 1	2 1 2 1	3 1 1	1 2 3	3 1 2	2 1 1 2	1 1
t h e r e	w e r e	a n d	y o u	a d d	i n t o	b e

LLL	LRL	LRL	RLLLLL	LLLL	LRL	RL
2 3 3	1 1 2	1 1 1	2 3 2 1 2 1	1 2 3 1	2 1 1	1 2
w a s	t h e	b u t	l e t t e r	d e a r	s i r	i s

Exercise III.

With the practice already acquired, you will be able to work out the most convenient fingering for this exercise for yourself.

Dear Sir. Yours truly. Faithfully yours. I am, dear madam. Yes, please. July 16th. January 1st, 1916. Thank you, sir, for your help. Good-bye. Good-morning. It's a fine day. I will call to-morrow (Wednesday) at 4-30. On Thursday, June 21st, at 12 o'clock. I can offer you £2 10s. 0d. per week. Thank you for your letter of yesterday's date.

After practising these phrases many times over, until you can do them automatically without stopping to think about the fingering, you will be able to go on to straight typing. Choose a fairly easy paragraph in a book or newspaper, and copy it as accurately as you can. Remember that the first line of a paragraph must always be indented —that is, it must start five spaces further to the right than the other lines. You will see what I mean by noticing the paragraphs on this page you are now reading.

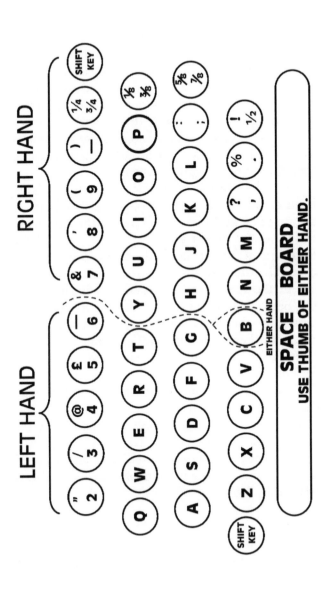

Another time type out a page or so from a story, choosing a part that has conversation in it. This will give you more practice in paragraphing, and also teach you the use of inverted commas.

Letters are such an important part of typewriting that you should take them next. Copy or invent any simple business letter and type it out as well as you can on a sheet of quarto paper, paying special attention to arrangement.

First, the address. Start this in the upper right-hand corner of the paper, typing the first letter of the first line at 40 on the indicator, the first letter of the second line at 45, and the first letter of the third line at 50. At 55 on the line below type the date. Then turn up from four to six lines, according to the length of the letter, and beginning at the beginning of the line, type the name of the person to whom you are writing. Underneath, five spaces further to the right for each line, comes his address. Then turn up four again, and write "Dear Sir" or "Dear Mr. Jones," with a comma after it. On the next line, ten spaces from the left-hand margin begin the letter.

Indent each new paragraph ten spaces. At the end of the letter, "Yours faithfully" or "Yours truly" comes on a line by itself, and begins at 35 or 40. Do not type any signature, as this is always written by hand.

Carbon Copies.

When one or more copies of any letter or other typewritten matter are required, these are usually obtained by employing carbons. In business houses carbon copies of all letters are usually taken, to keep for reference.

A carbon has one dull surface and one bright one. The dull surface must go next to the top sheet of paper, the bright side next to that on which the copy will appear.

The carbon between its two sheets of paper goes into the machine just as if it were only a single sheet. When inserting, the topmost typing sheet must be away from you, and the back of the under sheet towards you. To take two carbon copies at once, use another carbon and a third sheet of paper behind the second sheet. When a carbons are new three or four clear copies may be obtained. After several uses the carbons gradually become blurred, and when they cease to give clear duplicates they must be thrown away. When a carbon is nearly worn through you may give it a new lease of life by inserting it between the papers about half an inch lower than their top edges. This causes the keys to strike it in the comparatively untouched portions between the worn lines. When not in use carbons should be kept unfolded and flat.

RUBBING OUT.

Only special typewriter indiarubbers (costing 2d. each) must be used for erasing. The handiest shape is the circular kind with a hole in the middle. If you need to rub out when taking carbon copies, do not use the eraser on the top sheet just as it is, or the rubbing will cause the carbon to smear the under sheet. Slip a little bit of thin cardboard or thick paper between the top sheet and the carbon, just where the erasure will be, and rub out on this. Then turn up a few lines, lift up the top sheet and carbon, and make the erasure on the under sheet.

FIGURES AND SIGNS.

The figures 2 to 9 inclusive are found on the top row of keys on the standard keyboard. They belong to the lower case and are worked without the shift key. To get 1, use the small L and for nought, use a capital O.

The slanting stroke on the upper half of the 3 key is used for the date when written in this form: 1/1/16. It is also combined with the underline (over key 6) to form the omission mark / when a word or letter has been left out. Type the slanting stroke first, *then turn back* one to the same space and type the underline, when they will be found to join as above.

The underline is mainly used for underscoring words to give emphasis. When typing from printed matter, underscore all words which are printed in italics. First type the word, then go back to the space on which it begins, turn up the shift key, and use the underline under each letter of the word.

The mark % on the upper case above the full stop indicates the words per cent., and often occurs in financial or statistical typing. It is used for 10%, 20%, &c.

The extreme right-hand key of the lowest row on the standard keyboard usually serves for the exclamation mark above and the $\frac{1}{2}$ below. Sometimes, however, the upper sign is ..., and in this case the exclamation mark must be obtained by typing first the apostrophe (on the 8 key) and then the full stop on the same space.

As regards fractions, the halves, quarters and eighths are given on most keyboards. The thirds must be obtained with the help of the slanting line already referred to: thus, 1/3, 2/3.

The sign @ (at) on the upper half of the 4 key, is used only in making out invoices, and is incorrect elsewhere; thus, 1 dozen yards @ 6d. per yard.

The Care of a Typewriter.

The various tools required to keep a machine in good condition are generally supplied with it; they consist of a tiny oilcan containing typewriter or sewing machine oil, two brushes (a soft, long handled one, and another resembling a stiff, hard toothbrush), a pin or other pointed instrument for cleaning out type. Add to these a duster and a chamois leather.

A typewriter in regular use should be cleaned once a week. First dust it all over with a duster and the long-handled brush, which is specially adapted for getting into places the duster cannot reach; then rub up all the nickel parts of the machine (except the rods on which the carriage runs) with the chamois.

The rods, instead of being rubbed, should be wiped over with a rag moistened in typewriter oil. The machine must also be oiled—where, depends upon its construction and varies in different makes. Be sparing with the oil and wipe the machine carefully afterwards, or it may mark the paper next time you type.

Brush the type thoroughly with the stiff type brush, and clean out any clogged letters with a pin. Lastly, be careful to cover the typewriter whenever it is not in use.

INDEX